MEANS AND ENDS OF EDUCATION

First published 1895
This edition published by Lector House in 2024

ISBN: 978-93-6138-186-7

Lector House LLP
Registered Office: H. No. 96, Block C, Tomar Colony,
Burari, Delhi – 110084, India
info@lectorhouse.com
www.lectorhouse.com

MEANS AND ENDS OF EDUCATION

JOHN LANCASTER SPALDING

2024

LECTOR HOUSE LLP

MEANS AND ENDS OF EDUCATION

BY

J. L. SPALDING

Bishop of Peoria

WHO BRINGETH MANY THINGS,
FOR EACH ONE SOMETHING BRINGS

Contents

MEANS AND ENDS OF EDUCATION.

Chapter I.

Truth and Love.

None of us yet know, for none of us have yet been taught in early youth, what fairy palaces we may build of beautiful thought—proof against all adversity;—bright fancies, satisfied memories, noble histories, faithful sayings, treasure-houses of precious and restful thoughts; which care cannot disturb, nor pain make gloomy, nor poverty take away from us—houses built without hands for our souls to live in.—RUSKIN.

Stirred up with high hopes of living to be brave men and worthy patriots, dear to God and famous to all ages.—MILTON.

A great man's house is filled chiefly with menials and creatures of ceremony; and great libraries contain, for the most part, books as dry and lifeless as the dust that gathers on them: but from amidst these dead leaves an immortal mind here and there looks forth with light and love.

From the point of view of the bank president, Emerson tells us, books are merely so much rubbish. But in his eyes the flowers also, the flowing water, the fresh air, the floating clouds, children's voices, the thrill of love, the fancy's play, the mountains, and the stars are worthless.

Not one in a hundred who buy Shakspere, or Milton, or a work of any other great mind, feels a genuine longing to get at the secret of its power and truth; but to those alone who feel this longing is the secret revealed. We must love the man of genius, if we would have him speak to us. We learn to know ourselves, not by studying the behavior of matter, but through experience of life and intimate acquaintance with literature. Our spiritual as well as our physical being springs from that of our ancestors. Freedom, however, gives the soul the power not only to develop what it inherits, but to grow into conscious communion with the thought and love, the hope and faith of the noble dead, and, in thus enlarging itself, to become the inspiration and source of richer and wider life for those who follow. As parents are consoled by the thought of surviving in their descendants, great minds are upheld and strengthened in their ceaseless labors by the hope of entering as an added impulse to better things, from generation to generation, into the lives of thousands. The greatest misfortune which can befall genius is to be sold to the advocacy of what is not truth and love and goodness and beauty. The proper translation of *timeo hominem unius libri* is not, "I fear a man of one book," but "I dread a man of one book:" for he is sure to be narrow, one-sided, and unreasonable. The right phrase enters at once into our spiritual world, and its power becomes as real as that of material objects. The truth to which it gives body is borne in upon us as a star or a mountain is borne in upon us. Kings and rich men live in history when genius happens to throw the light of abiding worlds upon their ephemeral estate. Carthage is the typical city of merchants and traders. Why is it remembered? Because Hannibal was a warrior and Virgil a poet.

The strong man is he who knows how and is able to become and be himself; the magnanimous man is he who, being strong, knows how and is able to issue forth from himself, as from a fortress, to guide, protect, encourage, and save others. Life's current flows pure and unimpeded within him, and on its wave his thought and love are borne to bless his fellowmen. If he who gives a cup of water in the right spirit does God's work, so does he who sows or reaps, or builds or sweeps, or utters helpful truth or plays with children or cheers the lonely, or does any other fair or useful thing. Take not seriously one who treats with derision men or books that have been deemed worthy of attention by the best minds. He is false or foolish. As we cherish a human being for the courage and love he inspires, so books are dear to us for the noble thoughts and generous moods they call into being. To drink the spirit of a great author is worth more than a knowledge of his teaching.

He who desires to grow wise should bring his reason to bear habitually upon what he sees and hears not less than upon what he reads; for thus he soon comes to understand that whatever he thinks or feels, says or does, whatever happens within the sphere of his conscious life, may be made the means of self-improvement. "He is not born for glory," says Vauvenargues, "who knows not the worth of time." The educational value of books lies in their power to set the intellectual atmosphere in vibration, thereby rousing the mind to self-activity; and those which have not this power lack vitality.

If in a whole volume we find one passage in which truth is expressed in a noble and striking manner, we have not read in vain. To read with profit, we should read as a serious student reads, with the mind all alive and held to the subject; for reading is thinking, and it is valuable in proportion to the stimulus it gives to the exercise of faculty. The conversation of high and ingenuous minds is doubtless as instructive as it is delightful, but it is seldom in our power to call around us those with whom we should wish to hold discourse; and hence we go back to the emancipated spirits, who having transcended the bounds of time and space, are wherever they are desired and are always ready to entertain whoever seeks their company. Genius neither can nor will discover its secret. Why his thought has such a mould and such a tinge he no more knows than why the flowers have such a tint and such a perfume; and if he knew he would not care to tell. Nothing is wholly manifest. In the most trivial object, as in the simplest word, there lies a world of meaning which does not reveal itself to a passing glance. If therefore thou wouldst come to right understanding, consider all things with an awakened and interested curiosity.

When the mind at last finds itself rightly at home in its world, it is as delighted as children making escape from restraining walls, as full of spirit as colts newly turned upon the greensward.

In the realm of truth each one is king, and what he knows is as much his own as though he were its first discoverer. However firmly thou holdest to thy opinions, if truth appears on the opposite side, throw down thy arms at once. A book has the power almost of a human being to inspire admiration or disgust, love or hatred. To be useful is a noble thing, to be necessary is not desirable. The youth has not enough ambition unless he has too much. It is difficult to give lessons in the art of pleasing without teaching that of lying. The discouraged are already vanquished. In judging the deed let not the character of the doer influence thy opinion, for good is good, evil evil, by whomsoever done. When the author is rightly inspired his words need not interpretation. They are as natural and as beautiful as the faces of children or as new-blown flowers, and their meaning is plain. The spirit and love of dogmatism is characteristic of the imperfectly educated. As there is a communion of saints, there is a communion of noble minds, living and dead. To speak of love which is not felt, of piety which is not a living sentiment within us, is to weaken both in ourselves and in those who hear us the power of faith and affection. The best that has been known and experienced by minds and hearts lies asleep in books, ready to awaken for whoever holds the magician's wand. Books which at their first appearance create a breeze of excitement, are forgotten when the wind falls.

A human soul rightly uttering itself, in whatever age or country, ceases to belong to any age or country, and becomes part of the universal life of man. A sprightly wit may serve only to lead us astray, and to enmesh us more hopelessly in error. Deeper knowledge is the remedy for the foolishness of sciolism: like cures like. In the books in which men worth knowing have put some of the vital quality which makes them worth knowing, there is perennial inspiration. They are the form and substance of an immortal spirit which, in creating them, became itself. "I have not made my book," says Montaigne, "more than my book has made me."

Were one to ask an acquaintance who knows men to point out the individuals whom he should make his friends, his request would probably receive an unsatisfactory reply: for how, except by trial, is it possible to say who will suit whom? Those whose friendship would be valuable might, for whatever cause, be disagreeable to him, as the greatest and noblest may be unpleasant companions. Many a one whom we admire as he stands forth in history, whose words and deeds thrill and uplift us, we should detest had we known him in life; and others to whom we might have been drawn would have cared nothing for us. Between men and books there is doubtless a wide difference, though a good book contains the best of the life of some true man. But when we are asked to point out the books one should learn to love, we are confronted with much the same difficulty as had we been asked to name the persons whom he should make his friends. A book can have worth for us only when we have learned to love it; and since a real book, like a real man, has its proper character, it is not easy to determine whom it will please or displease. Once it has taken a safe place in literature, it will, of course, be praised by everybody; but this, like the praise of men, is often meaningless. All who read know something about the great books, but their knowledge, unless it leads them to intimate acquaintance with some one or several of these books, has little worth. Books are, indeed, a world which each one must discover for himself. Another may tell us about them, but the truth and beauty there is in them for each one, each one must find. The value of a book, like that of a man, lies not in its freedom from fault, but in its qualities, in the good it contains. Words which inspire the love of spiritual beauty and noble action cannot be false: the consent of the wise places them in the canon. The imperishable goods are truth, freedom, love, and beauty. Valuable alone is that which enriches and ennobles life. There are natures for whom the lack of knowledge is as painful as the lack of food. They are ahungered and athirst for it, and their suffering impels them to ceaseless meditation and study, as the only means of relief.

The self-educator's first and simplest aim should be to learn to know and do well whatever he knows and does; and to this end let him often observe and consider how rare are they who know anything thoroughly or do well any of the hundred things which are part of daily life: who talk well, or write well, or behave well. Herbert Spencer affirms that it is better to learn the meanings of things than the meanings of words; but he loses sight of the fact that the meanings of things become plain only when things are clothed in words, which, in truth, are things, being nothing else than the very form and body of nature as it reveals itself within the mind of man. The world is chiefly a mental fact. From mind it receives the forms of time and space, the principle of causality, color, warmth, and beauty. Were there no mind, there would be no world. The end of man is the pursuit of perfection, through communion with God, his fellows, and nature, by means of knowledge and conduct, of faith, hope, admiration, and love. It is easy to praise work overmuch. Like money, it is a means, not an end, and it is good or evil as it is made to help or harm the worker, for man is an end, not a means. The work which millions are still forced to do is a curse,—the trail of the serpent is over it all, and no people has the right to call itself civilized, while work which dehumanizes is not merely permitted, but encouraged.

Let us not teach the young to believe they are born into a world of delights and pleasures, but let us strive to enable them to realize that, upon this earth, only the wise and good and strong can make themselves really at home; that for the wicked and the weak its very delights and pleasures turn to sorrow and suffering. We pity the hard-driven beast of burden. How then is it possible to look with complacency on a world in which multitudes of human beings are condemned to the work of the ox and the ass? For the healthy man, wealth and happiness would seem to be identical, if his desires are confined to the things of which money is the equivalent. But this is a delusion, for the plenary possession of these things has never satisfied a human being. Man needs virtue, knowledge, love, and to take the obvious view, he needs the power to enjoy the things money buys; and of this money deprives him.

When we consider the many unworthy means men take to gain wealth and office, we are forced to believe that to reach their ends they are ready to profess to hold opinions and beliefs about which they care nothing or which they really do not accept at all. By this following of time-servers and place-hunters every noble cause is weakened and the purest faith is corrupted.

To labor for those we love, to sit in the hours of rest, with wife and children about us, smiling in the blaze of the fire we have lighted, sheltered by the roof we have built, secure in the sense of protection our presence inspires, is to feel that life is good. But is it not a higher thing to turn away, in disrespect of all this peace and comfort, and to strive alone, by thought and deed, to find the way which leads to God and to be a pioneer therein for those who wander helpless and astray? The more we dwell with truth and love, the more conscious we become that they are the best, and are everlasting; and thus our immortality is revealed to us. Visibly we float on the boundless stream and disappear; but inasmuch as we are truth-loving and love-cherishing, we dwell in an abiding city, and may behold our bodies carried forth by the flood, as a man sees his house swept away, while he himself remains. Our thoughtlessness and indifference, our indolence and frivolousness, blind us to the infinite worth and significance of life; and they who call themselves religious often take it as lightly as worldlings and unbelievers.

In the Universe there is nothing which exists separate and apart from other things. The satellites hold to the planets, the planets to the suns, the suns to one another, all in obedience to the same laws which bind the body to earth, and cause the water to flow and the vapor to rise. For the senses there is separateness, but for the mind there is union and unity. Communion is the law of souls as of bodies. Both are immersed in a boundless world, from which if they could be drawn forth they would cease to be. The principle of this infinite harmony is love, is God.

The right human bond is that which unites soul with soul; and only they are truly akin who consciously live in the same world, who think, believe, and love alike, who hope for the same things, aspire to the same ends.

Our mental view never reaches the ultimate nature of being, and hence our knowledge, whether of material or of spiritual things, is incomplete. Faith is the effort to supply the defect which inheres in all our knowing. Knowledge springs from faith, faith from knowledge, as rivers from clouds, clouds from rivers. The more we know, the more we believe; and our growing consciousness does not make us content to rest in a mechanical view of nature, but it brings home to us with increasing power the awfulness of the infinite mystery, which we more and more clearly perceive to be a spiritual rather than a material fact. If at present there is a certain failure of will and consequent discouragement in the pursuit of moral and intellectual perfection, this is a result of our passing bewilderment in the presence of the revelations of science and of the mighty forces it places in the hands of man, and not of any new knowledge which tends to inspire misgivings concerning the being of God and our kinship with Him:—-

From nature up to law, from law to love:
This is the ascendant path in which we move,
Impelled by God in ways that lighten still,
Till all things meet in one eternal thrill.

As the Universe revealed by the Copernican astronomy and the other natural sciences is infinitely more sublime and marvellous than such a world as the Israelites, the Greeks, or the Romans imagined, so they who see rightly in the luminous ether of modern intelligence understand better than the ancients that human life is not an ephemeral and superficial, but an immortal and central power, enrooted in God, and drawing its substance and sustenance from Him.

The appeal to shame is a poor argument. The fact that men of great intellectual power and learning have held an opinion to be true does not make it so. New knowledge may have shown it to be false, or the general advance of the race may have changed the point of view. The presumption of the larger wisdom of the Ancients we cannot accept: for we, not they, are the true ancients. The purest and the holiest prayer men speak is this: “Thy will be done.” They who utter it from the inmost soul, find peace, even as a fretful child sinks to rest upon the mother’s bosom. In learning to love the will of

God they come at last not merely to believe, but to feel that His will guides the Universe, and that all will be well. When an utterance comes forth from the depths of our spiritual being, men cannot but hearken. It is as though we should bring to exiles tidings of a long-lost home and country.

To what a weight he stoops who addresses himself with fixed resolve to the life of thought! The burden indeed is heavy, but the pathway lies through pleasant fields where great souls move to and fro in freedom and at peace. And as he grows accustomed to his labor, the world widens, the heavens break open, the dead live again, and with them he rises into the high regions where the petty cares and passions of mortals do not reach.

He who would educate himself must make use of his own powers. He must observe, think, examine, read, argue, ponder; he must learn when to hold judgment in suspense, and when to give the wings of the soul free sweep through the high and serene realms of truth and beauty. The farther we dwell from the crowd, with its current opinion, the better and truer shall we and our thoughts become. They who write for multitudinous readers rise with difficulty above the dignity of mountebanks.

There is a radical defect in the character of whoever works in the spirit of a trifler, however blameless his conduct. The power to inspire faith in the seriousness and goodness of life is a sufficient test of the worth of a scheme of education.

No one should fill an office which he is unable to hold without hindrance to the play of mind and heart that makes him a man. The dignities we possess at the cost of knowledge and virtue are like jewels for the sake of which one goes hungry and naked; mere glittering baubles for which we barter the soul's prosperity.

Experience is personal, and it is largely incommunicable; but genius—and in this lies its power and charm—renders it communicable. What the poet or the painter has felt and seen, he makes all men feel and see. The difference between man and man, between the child and the youth, the youth and the adult, is chiefly a difference in feeling, in the manner in which they are impressed; and it is our nature to be drawn in admiration or reverence to those who by their words or deeds give us deeper impressions of the worth of life, and thus open for us new sources of feeling.

Fair thoughts rise in the heart and mind of genius, like the fragrant breath which the dewy flowers exhale in the face of the rising sun, and they utter themselves as simply as matin songs warbled by sweet-throated birds.

Faith in the infinite nature and worth of truth, goodness, and love, is the dawn which shall merge into the fulness of day, when, in other worlds, God looks upon the soul, reborn from out this seemingness.

Our position, our reputation, our wealth, our comforts, are but a vesture like the body itself. They shall fall away, and we shall remain with God. There is no liberty but obedience to the impulse of the higher nature which urges us to think nobly, to act rightly, and to love constantly. The dominion of appetite is slavery; the dominion of reason and conscience is freedom.

Renan somewhere says he could wish for nothing better than that a little volume of selections from his writings might commend itself to young women, whose fair faces should bend over it, and find there a reflection of their own pure souls. But where there is no God, the soul is not mirrored, and we never really love an author who weakens faith and hope.

With whatever success we advance towards the wide and serene life of the pure reason, let us still cling to faith, hope, and love, the primal powers which keep watch at our birth, and which bend over our cradles, and which alone lift us into the world of enduring peace and hold us within the sheltering arms of God. In the enlightened mind, faith is a higher virtue than it can be for the ignorant, and to sustain it there is need of a nobler life.

He whom neither learning nor power nor wealth can corrupt must have virtue; for learning breeds conceit, and power begets pride, and wealth debases both the mind and heart.

The intellect does not recognize that conscience may forbid its exercise, since knowledge cannot be evil. If earth were a hell and life a curse and the Universe but a cinder, it would still be good to know the fact. The saddest truth is better than the merriest lie.

To know a thing is to be conscious of its relation to the mind. We know it, not in itself, but in and through this relation. Our knowledge of God, who is the absolute, is not absolute knowledge, but a knowledge of Him in so far as He is related to the mind of man. Since, however, mind is reason and not unreason, there is harmony between it and things, between it and God; and hence to be conscious of its relation to God and the universe is to be conscious of a real relation, in which both the thinker and his thought are in truth what they seem to be. The ultimate reality is inferred, not directly perceived. It reveals itself to the purest faith and love, and may be hidden from one who knows all the sciences.

As man's relations to his fellows make him a social and political being, so his relations to the unseen power behind and within the visible world, of whose presence he is always, however dimly, conscious, and to whom he refers whatever touches the senses, as well as the principle of life itself, make him a religious being.

In identifying what seem to be our particular interests with the interests of all, we make escape from narrowness and isolation into the general life of humanity; and when we come to understand that not only mankind but all nature is a Unity in the Consciousness of the Infinite and Eternal, bound together by thought and love, we enter into the glorious liberty of the Sons of God, and feel that nor height nor depth nor things past nor things to come shall separate us from the divine charity. We are akin to all that may become part of our life; and whatever we know or love or admire is spiritualized and made human. To understand the things of the spirit we must have spiritual experience. The intuitions of time and space, as well as the principle of causality, are given in the constitution of the mind. So is the idea of being, of perfection, of beauty, of eternity, of infinity, of duty. To think implies being, to perceive things as existing in time and space implies consciousness of eternity and infinity. To know the imperfect is possible only in the light of the perfect. Subject is itself object, the first known and best understood, and the laws of mind are laws of being. If the constitution of mind makes the revelation of the material world possible only under the forms of time and space, intelligible only as sequence of cause and effect, the reason is to be found in the nature of things. If the constitution of mind postulates one who knows and shapes, in a world in which whatever is, is intelligible, in which there is order, proportion, and purpose, it is because such an One is given in the nature of things, and He is God. However living our faith, it is faith and not knowledge; and should it become knowledge, it would cease to be faith.

There are three kinds of authors,—those who impart knowledge, those who give delight, and those who strengthen and inspire.

A noble thought rightly expressed sweeps the higher nerve centres as the touch of a perfect performer the strings of an instrument; but if the instrument is poor and irresponsive, the appeal is made in vain. Life has the power to propagate itself, and if the words thou utterest are living, they will strike root somewhere and bud and blossom and bear fruit; but if there is no life in them, be content to have them fall and lie amid the dust of the dead. God and the universe are what they are, and the best even genius can do is to throw over them a revealing light. He who feels that he is always in the presence of God will strive as religiously to think only what is true as he will strive to do only what is right. A phrase which leaps forth aglow with life from the heart and brain of genius, not only lives forever, but retains forever the power to awaken, when brought into contact with a brain and heart, the thrill with which it first came into being.

Only a few know and love the poet, but they are young and fair, and the music of high thoughts and pure love is rhythmic with the current of their blood; and if among them there be found some who are old, they are choice spirits who have risen from out the lapses of time into regions where what is true and beautiful is so forever. This little band of chosen ones accompanies him adown the centuries, and listens to the melody which wells in his heart and breaks into songs that shall give delight as long as the air of spring is pleasant and the flowers fragrant and the carollings of birds delightful; and while the poet strolls on the outskirts of time, thus loved and thus attended, the stormy and glittering favorites of the crowd drop from sight and are forgotten, or remembered but as the echo of a name.

A line from Homer, which sounds like a response from our own heart, is clothed with the mystery of diviner power, because it makes us feel that we were alive thousands of years ago amid the Grecian isles, thus revealing to us the unreality of time and space, and the everlasting nature of truth and beauty.

As it is right to admire and love whatever is good wherever it is found, it needs must be the part of wisdom to seek to know and appreciate all that is true and high in the works of genius, though there, like precious stones and metals in the mine, it be mingled with baser matter. It is but narrowness or intellectual pharisaism to turn from a great author because in his life and works there may be things of which we cannot approve. Shall we abandon God because His world is full of evil, or Christ because there is corruption in the church? St. Paul appeals to pagan literature, St. Augustine is the disciple of Plato, St. Thomas Aquinas of Aristotle, and the culture and civilization of Christendom are largely due to influences which are not Christian.

Whatever is good is from God. There is no surer mark of the lack of culture than the use of ill-natured and abusive epithets. To feel the need of injurious words to express one's opinion, merely shows that one is angry, and anger is vulgar.

Whatever is inspired by vanity is in bad taste. This is why a showy style is a false style, why fine writing is poor writing. The author yields to the spirit of vainglory, whereas he should be wholly bent upon uttering his thought as he knows it. It is as though he should call our attention to a costly garb when what we want to see is a man.

As a plain face is better than a mask, though fine, so one's own style, though inferior, is better than any which is borrowed.

True books survive without help or let of critics, by virtue of their vital quality, which attracts kindred spirits with irresistible power.

When their worth becomes known, the critics set up a howl of praise, and many buy; but only a few make them their serious study, and learn to know and love them. Truth is the mind's food; and, like that of the body, it is nourishment only when it has been digested and assimilated. It is, after all, but a little while since man began to think. As yet he is learning the alphabet. Take heart then, and apply thy mind. As we grow older the years seem to run to months, the months to weeks, the weeks to days, the days to hours, the hours to moments, until time, like an exhalation, appears to dissolve in the inane, and become the nothing it was and is and will be for eternity.

If thought were given us, like house and clothing, merely for our personal comfort, wisdom would lead us to think with and like all the world. They who are eager for the good opinion of others seem to have but weak faith in their own worth.

The art of pleasing would better deserve our study were there more who are worth pleasing, or were it less difficult to please without loss of sincerity and without stooping to the service of vulgar interests. Not how much or how many things thou knowest is of import. An industrious reader, of retentive memory, will easily know more things than a great philosopher compared with whom he is but a child.

Know thyself was the sum of what Socrates taught, and each of the seven wise men rested his fame upon an apothegm. To expect the multitude to appreciate the best in life or literature, is to expect them to be what they have never been and will probably never be. Would you have an ox admire the sunrise or the pearly dew, when all he feels the need of is grass? Appeal to the many if you will, but if your appeal is for the highest, only the few will hearken.

Consider not what great men or books are worth in themselves, but what they are worth to thee; for thou art able to judge of their value only in so far as thou understandest and lovest them.

If thou canst not bear trouble, sorrow, and disappointment without loss of composure, thou art poorly equipped for life's struggle. If thou mayst not lead the life thou wouldst wish, thou canst at least make the life thou leadest the means to improve thyself. If we were so constituted that thought, feeling, and imagination might have free and healthful play in ever-during darkness and isolation, life would still be good. Could I live surrounded by those I love, I should feel less keenly the discontent which the consciousness of my higher needs creates; and besides, it is not easy to rest in the comforts and luxuries which make and keep us inferior, except in the company of those we love. If our ordinary power of sight were as great as that we gain with the help of the microscope, the world would become for us a place of horrors; and if we could clearly see ourselves as we are, life would be less endurable. God blurs our vision as a mother hides from her child its wound.

Pleasures which quickly end in revulsion of feeling are but momentary escapes from pain; and they alone are fortunate who are able to persevere in pursuits which give them pure delight. "All good," says Kant, "which is not based on the highest moral principle is but empty appearance and splendid misery."

Sensations of color, taste, sound, smell, touch, heat and cold, perceptions of magnitude, and temporal and spatial relations, is the sum of what we know; and yet we are conscious that reason means infinitely more than this, that its proper object is the eternal world of truth, goodness, and beauty. Think for thyself with a single view to truth; for so only will thy thought be of worth and service to others. We feel ourselves only in action, and hence the need of doing lest we lose ourselves and be swallowed in nothingness. And for the old and feeble even worry, I suppose, is a comfort, for it helps to keep this self-consciousness alive. It is impossible to say whence a thought comes, and it is often difficult to determine the occasion by which it has been suggested.

Fortunate are the children all of whose knowledge comes from man and nature in their purity, whose memory holds no words which are not the symbols of what they themselves have seen and felt, in whose minds no will-o'-the-wisp from chimera worlds flits to and fro. It is only by keeping men in ignorance and vice that it is possible to keep them from the contagion of great thoughts. They who have little are thought to have no right to anything. Thus the plagiarized sayings of Napoleon and other nurslings of fame pass for their own; who their real authors were, seeming to be a matter of indifference.

If I am not pleased with myself, but should wish to be other than I am, why should I think highly of the influences which have made me what I am? Should I publish what I believe to be true and well expressed, and competent judges should declare it to be worthless in form and substance, the verdict would be interesting to me, and I should set to work to discover why and how I had so far failed in discernment. "A thoroughly cultivated man," says Fontenelle, "is informed by all the thinkers of the past, as though he had lived and continued to grow in knowledge during all the centuries." The author is rewarded when his readers are made better.

The most persuasive of men are the praisers of patent medicines. Their eloquence is more richly rewarded than that of all the orators, who also are paid, for the most part, in inverse ratio to the amount of truth they utter. Fame, as fame, is the merest vanity. No wise man wishes to be talked and written about, living or dead, to be a theme chiefly for fools.

Literature is writing in which genuine thought and feeling are rightly expressed. They who content themselves with what others have uttered, learn nothing. The blind need a guide, but they who are able to see should look for themselves. There is, indeed, in the words of genius a glow which never dies; but it only dazzles and misleads, if it fails to stimulate and strengthen our own powers of vision. True speech is not idle; it is utterance of life, the mate of action, and the begetter of noble deeds. Strive for knowledge and strength, but do not appear to have them.

"A book," says La Bruyère, "which exalts the mind and inspires high and manly thoughts, is good, and the work of a master." A phrase suffices to tell the man is ignorant or the book worthless. As the body is nourished by dead things, vegetable and animal, so the mind feeds on the thoughts of those who have ceased to live, which, it would seem, are never rightly understood until the thinkers have passed away.

To be unwilling to be proved wrong is to fail in love of truth; to resent an objection is to lack culture. One may believe what cannot be demonstrated, but to grow angry because there is no proof is absurd.

To do deeds and to utter thoughts which long after we have departed shall remain to cheer, to illumine, to strengthen and console, is to be like God; and the desire of noble minds is not of praise, but of abiding power for good.

He who is certain of himself needs not the good opinion of men, not of those even who are competent to judge. Only the vain and foolish or the designing and dishonest will wish to receive credit for more ability and virtue than they have. An exaggerated reputation may nourish conceit or win favor; but the wise and the good put away conceit, and desire not favors which are granted from mistaken notions.

"I hate false words," says Landor, "and seek with care, difficulty, and moroseness those that fit the thing."

Dwell not with complacency upon aught thou hast or hast achieved, but address thyself each day, like a simple-hearted child, to the task God sets thee; and remember when the last hour comes thou canst carry nothing to Him but faith in His mercy and goodness.

Chapter II.

Truth and Love.

> Truth, which only doth judge itself, teacheth that the inquiry of truth, which is the love-making or wooing of it; the knowledge of truth, which is the presence of it; and the belief of truth, which is the enjoying of it, is the sovereign good of human nature.
>
> —Bacon.

As those who have little think their little much, so those who have few ideas believe with obstinacy that they are the sum of all truth. If the world could but be made to see what they see there would be no ills. They have not even a suspicion of the unutterable complexity of the warp and woof of nature and of life; and when their opinions are combated they imagine they thereby acquire new importance, and they defend them with such zeal that they make proselytes and found sects in religion, politics, and literature. The source of the greater part of error is the absoluteness the mind attributes to its knowledge and, as part of this, the persuasion that at each stage of our mental life, we are capable of seeing things as they are. The aim of the philosopher, as of the Christian, is to escape from the ephemeral self by renouncing what is petty, partial, apparent, and transitory, that the true self may unfold in the world of the permanent, of things which have an aptitude for perpetuity; but the philosopher's efforts are intellectual and moral, while the Christian's source of strength is the love which is enrooted in divine faith.

"The brief precept," says St. Augustine, "is given there once for all,—Love, and do what thou wilt. If thou art silent, be silent for love; if thou speakest, speak for love; if thou correctest, correct for love; if thou sparest, spare for love. The root of love is within, and from it only good can come." Life springs from love, and love is its being, aim, and end. Each soul is born of souls yearning that he be born, and he lives only so far as he leaves himself and becomes through love part of the life of God and the race of man.

Primordial matter, with which the physicists start, is twin brother of nothing. In every conceivable hypothesis, we assume either that nothing is the cause of something, or that from the beginning there was something or some one who is all the universe may become. If truth and love and goodness are of the essence of the highest life evolved in nature, they are of the essence of that by which nature exists and energizes. If reason is valid at all, it avails as an immovable foundation for faith in God and in man's kinship with him. The larger the world we live in, the greater the opportunities for self-education. He who knows friends and foes, who is commended and found fault with, who tastes the delights of home and breathes the air of strange lands, who is followed and opposed, who triumphs and suffers defeat, who contends with many and is left alone, who dwells with his own thoughts and in the company of the great minds of all time,—necessarily gains wisdom and power, and learns to feel himself a man.

Science springs from man's yearning for truth; art, from his yearning for beauty; religion, from his yearning for love: and as truth, beauty, and love are a harmony, so are science, art, and religion; and if conflicts arise, they are the results of ignorance and passion. The charm of faith, hope, and love, of knowledge, beauty, and religion, lies in their power to open life's prison, thus permitting the soul to escape to commune with the Infinite and Eternal, with the boundless mysterious world of being which forever draws us on and forever eludes our grasp. The higher the man, the more urgent this need of self-escape.

We look upon lifelong imprisonment of the body as among the greatest of evils, but that the mind should be suffered to languish in the dungeon of ignorance, error, and prejudice, seems comparatively a slight thing. Thy whole business, as a rational being, is to know and follow truth,—with gratitude and joy if possible, but, in any case, with courage and resignation. Mind maketh man; and the most money and place can do, is to make millionnaires and titularies.

The Alpine guides, who lead travellers through the sublimest scenery in the world, are as insensible to its grandeur as the stocks they grasp; and we nearly all are as indifferent as these drudges to Nature's divine spectacle, with its starlit heavens, its risings and settings of sun and moon, its storms and calms, its changes of season, its clouds and snows and breath of many-tinted flowers, its children's faces, and plumage and songs of birds.

As we judge of many things by samples, a glance may suffice to show the worthlessness of a book, but the value of one that is genuine is not quickly perceived, for it reveals itself the more the oftener it is read and pondered. There is not a more certain, a purer, or a more delightful source of contentment and independence than a taste for the best literature. In the midst of occupations and cares of whatever kind it enables us to look forward to the hour when the noblest minds and most generous hearts shall welcome us to their company to be entertained with great thoughts rightly uttered and with information concerning whatever is of interest to man.

In every home the best works of the great poets, historians, philosophers, orators, and story-writers should lie within reach of the young, who should be permitted, not urged, to read them. We may know a man by the company he keeps; we may know him better still by the books he loves: and if he loves none, he is not worth knowing.

Matthew Arnold praises culture for "its inexhaustible indulgence, its consideration of circumstances, its severe judgment of actions joined to its merciful judgment of persons."

When we have learned to love work, to love honest work, work well done, excellently well done, we have within ourselves the most fruitful principle of education.

Who shall speak ill of bodily health and vigor? Herbert Spencer affirms that it is man's first duty to be a good animal. But since we cannot all be athletes or be well even, let us not refuse to find consolation in the fact that much of what is greatest, whether in the world of thought or action, has been wrought by mighty souls in feeble and suffering bodies; and since men gladly risk health and life to acquire gold, shall we not be willing, if need be, to be "sicklied o'er with the pale cast of thought," if so we may attain to truth and love?

Great things are accomplished only by concentration. What we ourselves think, love, and do, until it becomes a habit, is the form and substance of our life.

To live in the company of those who have or seek culture is to breathe the vital air of mental health and vigor.

The scientific investigator gives his whole attention to the facts before him; but the discipline of close observation, however favorable it may be to accuracy, weakens capacity for wide and profound views. On the other hand, the speculative thinker is apt to grow heedless or oblivious of facts. Hence a minute observer is seldom a great philosopher, a great philosopher rarely a careful observer.

"Employment," says Ruskin, "is the half, and the primal half of education, for it forms the habits of body and mind, and these are the constitution of man." Tell me at and in what thou workest, and I will tell thee what thou art. The secret of education lies in the words of Christ,—He that hath eyes to see, let him see; he that hath ears to hear, let him hear. The soul must flow through the channels of the senses until it meets the universe and clothes it with the beauty and meaning which reveal God.

When I think of all the truth which still remains for me to learn, of all the good I yet may do, of all the friends I still may serve, of all the beauty I may see, life seems as fresh and fair, as full of promise, as is to loving souls the dawn of their bridal day. Animals, children, savages, the thoughtless and frivolous, live in the present alone; they consequently lead a narrow, ephemeral, and superficial existence. They strike no deep roots into the past, they forebode no divine future, they enter not behind the veil where the soul finds ever-during truth and power.

> "The world is too much with us; late and soon,
> Getting and spending, we lay waste our powers."

Whatever sets the mind in motion may lead us to secret worlds, though it be a falling apple, as with Newton, or the swing of the pendulum, as with Galileo, or a boy's kite, as with Franklin, or throwing pebbles into the water, as with Turner. Watt sat musing by the fire, and noticed the rise and fall of the lid of the boiling kettle, and the steam engine, like a vision from unknown spheres, rose before his imagination. A child, carelessly playing with the glasses that lay on the table of a spectacle-maker, gave the clew to the invention of the telescope. The pestle, flying from the hand of Schwarz, told him he had found the explosive which has transformed the world. Drifting plants, of a strange species, whispered to Columbus of a continent that lay across the Atlantic. Patient observation and work are the mightiest conquerors.

Among the maxims, called triads, which have come down to us from the Celtic bards, we find this: "The three primary requisites of genius,—an eye that can see nature; a heart that can feel nature; and boldness that dares follow nature." He who has no philosophy and no religion, no theory of life and the world, has nothing which he finds it greatly important to say or do. He lacks the impulse of genius, the educator's energy and enthusiasm. Having no ideal, he has no end to which he may point and lead. To do well it is necessary to believe in the worth of what we do. The power which upholds and leads us on is faith,—faith in God, in ourselves, in life, in education.

Forever to be blessed and cherished is the love-inspired mother or the teacher whose generous heart and luminous mind first leads us to believe in the priceless worth of wisdom and virtue, thus kindling within the soul a quenchless fire which warms and irradiates our whole being.

To be God's workman, to strive, to endure, to labor, even to the end, for truth and righteousness, this is life.

"My desire," says Dante, "and my will rolled onward, like a wheel in even motion, swayed by the love which moves the sun and all the stars."

If there are any who shrink from wrong more than from disgrace they best deserve to be called religious.

Strive not to be original or profound, but to think justly and to express clearly what thou seest; and so it may happen that thy view shall pierce deeper than thou knowest.

The words and deeds which are most certain to escape oblivion are those which nourish the higher life of the soul. Self-love, the love of one's real self, of one's soul, is the indispensable virtue. It is this we seek when we strive to know and love truth and justice; it is this we seek, when we love God and our fellow-men. In turning from ourselves to find them, we still seek ourselves; in abandoning life we seek richer and fuller life.

Truth separate from love is but half truth. Think of that which unites thee with thy fellows rather than of what divides thee from them. Religion is the bond of love, and not a subject for a debating club. If thou wouldst refute thy adversaries, commit the task to thy life more than to thy words. Read the history of controversy and ask thyself whether there is in it the spirit of Christ, the meek and lowly One? Its champions belong to the schools of the sophists rather than to the worshippers of God in spirit and in truth. And what has been the issue of all their disputes but hatreds and sects, persecutions and wars? If it is my duty to be polite and helpful to my neighbor, it is plainly also my duty to treat his opinions and beliefs with consideration and fairness.

There is a place in South America where the whole population have the goitre, and if a stranger who is free from the deformity chances to pass among them, they jeer and cry, "There goes one who has no goitre." What could be more delightfully human? We think it a holy thing to put down duelling, the battle of one with one; but we are full of enthusiasm over battles of a hundred thousand with a hundred thousand. Thus the Southern slave-owners were sworn advocates of the rights of man and of popular liberty.

The explanation of many provoking things is to be found in Dr. Johnson's words,—"Ignorance, simple ignorance;" but of many more probably in these other words,—Greed, simple greed.

"In science," says Bulwer, "read by preference the newest books; in literature, the oldest." This is wiser than Emerson's saying: "Never read a book which is not a year old."

The facility with which it is now possible to get at whatever is known on any subject has a tendency to create the opinion that reading up in this or that direction is education, whereas such reading as is generally done, is unfavorable to discipline of mind. Shall our Chautauquas and summer schools help to foster this superstition?

What passion can be more innocent than the passion for knowledge? And what passion gives better promise of blessings to one's self and to one's fellow-men? Why desire to have force and numbers on thy side? Is it not enough that thou hast truth and justice?

The loss of the good opinion of one's friends is to be regretted, but the loss of self-respect is the only true beggary.

Zeal for a party or a sect is more certain of earthly reward than zeal for truth and religion.

As it is unfortunate for the young to have abundance of money, fine clothes, and social success, so popularity is hurtful to the prosperity of the best gifts. It draws the mind away from the silence and strength of eternal truth and love into a world of clamor and noise. Patience is the student's great virtue; it is the mark of the best quality of mind. It takes an eternity to unfold a universe; man is the sum of the achievements of innumerable ages, and whatever endures is slow in acquiring the virtues which make for permanence.

The will to know, manifesting itself in persistent impulse, in never-satisfied yearning, is the power which urges to mental effort and enables us to attain culture.

"If a thing is good," says Landor, "it may be repeated. The repetition shows no want of invention; it shows only what is uppermost in the mind, and by what the writer is most agitated and inflamed." What hast thou learned to admire, to long for, to love, genuinely to hope for and believe? The answer tells thy worth and that of the education thou hast received.

When we have said a thousand things in praise of education, we must, at last, come back to the fundamental fact that nearly everything depends on the kind of people of whom we are descended, and on the kind of family in which our young years have passed. Nearly everything, but not everything; and it is this little which makes liberty possible, which inspires hope and courage, which, like the indefinable something that gives the work of genius its worth and stamp, makes us children of God and masters of ourselves. "Wisdom is the principal thing," says Solomon; "therefore get wisdom, and with all thy getting, get understanding."

He who makes himself the best man is the most successful one, while he who gains most money or notoriety may fail utterly as man.

With the advance of civilization our wants increase; and yet it is the business of religion and culture to raise us above the things money buys, and consequently to diminish our wants. They who are nearest to God have fewest wants; and they who know and follow truth need not place or title or wealth.

To every one the tempter comes, with a thousand pretexts drawn both from the intellect and the emotional nature, promising to lull conscience to sleep that he may lead the lower life in peace; but he who hearkens becomes a victim as helpless and as wretched as the victims of alcohol and opium.

In deliberate persevering action for high ends, all the subconscious forces within us, the many currents, which, like hidden water-veins, go to make our being, are taken up and turned in a deep-flowing stream into the ocean of our life. In such course of conduct the baser self is swallowed, and we learn to feel that we are part of the divine energy which moves the universe to finer issues. As life is only by moments and in narrow space, a little thing may disturb us and a little thing may take away the cause of our trouble. We are petty beings in a world of petty concerns. A little food, a little sleep, a little joy is enough to make us happy. A word can fill us with dismay, a breath can blow out the flickering flame of our self-consciousness. I often ride among graves, and think how easy it is for the fretful children of men to grow quiet. There they lie, having become weary of their toys and plays, on the breast of the great mother from whom they sprang, about whose face they frolicked and fought and cried for a day, and then fell back into her all-receiving arms, as raindrops fall into the water and mingle with it and are lost. No sight is so pathetic as that of a vast throng seeking to enjoy themselves. The hopelessness of the task is visible on all their thousand faces, athwart which, while they talk or listen or look, the shadow of care flits as if thrown from dark wings wheeling in circuits above them. The sorrow and toil and worry they have thought to put away, still lie close to them, like a burden which, having been set down, waits to be taken up again. God surely sees with love and pity His all-enduring and all-hoping children; it is His voice we hear in the words of Christ, "Misereor super turbam." I cannot but wish to be myself, and therefore to be happy; but when I think of God as essential to my happiness, I feel it is enough for me to know and love Him; for to imagine I might be of service to Him would be the fondest conceit. But He makes it possible for me to help my fellows, and in doing this, I fulfil the will of Him who is the father of all. The divine reveals itself in the human; and that religion alone is true which, striking its roots deep into humanity, exerts all its power to make men more godlike by making them more human.

They who in good faith inflicted the tortures of the Inquisition were led not by the light of reason, or that which springs from the contemplation of the life of Christ, but by the notion that the rack and fagot are instruments of mercy, if employed to save men from eternal torments; and tyrants, who are always cruel, gave encouragement and aid to the victims of fanaticism. Why should the sorrow or the sin or the loss of any human being give me pleasure? Is it not always the same story? In the fall of one we all are degraded, since, whoever fails, it is our common nature which suffers hurt.

Whether or not we have come forth from a merely animal condition, let us thank God we are human, and bend all our energies to remove the race farther and farther from the life over which thought and love and conscience have no dominion.

In the presence of the mighty machine, whose wheels and arms are everywhere, whose power is drawn from the exhaustless oceans and the boundless heavens, the importance of the individual dwindles and seems threatened with extinction. At such a time it is good to know that a right human soul is greater than a universe of machinery.

We feel that we are higher than all the suns and planets, because we know and love, and they do not; but when, in the light of this superiority, we turn to the thought of our own littleness, being scarcely more than nothing, such trouble rises in the soul that we throw ourselves upon God to escape doubt of the reality of life. If we believe that man is what he eats, his education is simply a question of alimentation; but if we hold that he is what he knows, and loves, and yearns, and strives for, his education is a problem of soul-nutrition.

The child is made educable by its faith in the father and mother, which is nothing else than faith in their truth and love; and the educableness of the man is in proportion to his faith in the sovereign and infinite nature of truth and love, which is faith in God.

It is in youth that we are most susceptible of education, because it is the privilege of youth to be free from tyrannic cares, and to be sensitive to the charm of noble and disinterested passions. If we show the young soul the way to higher worlds, he will not ask us to strew it with flowers, or pave it with gold, but he will be content to walk with bruised feet along mountain wastes, if at the summit is illumination and joy and peace.

As in religion many are called but few chosen, as in the race for wealth and place many start but few win the prize, so in the pursuit of intellectual and moral excellence, of the few who begin, the most soon weary, while of the remnant, many grow infirm in purpose or in body before the goal is reached.

Time and space, which hold all things, separate all things; but religion and culture bind them into unity through faith in God and through knowledge, thus forming a communion of holy souls and noble minds, for whom discord and division disappear in the harmony of the divine order in which temporal and spatial conditions of separateness yield to the eternal presence of truth and love. New ideas seem at first to remain upon the surface of the soul, and generations sometimes pass before they enter into its substance and become motives of conduct; and, in the same way, sentiments may influence conduct, when the notions from which they sprang have long been rejected. The old truth must renew itself as the race renews itself; it must be re-interpreted and re-applied to the life of each individual and of each generation, if its liberating and regenerating power is to have free scope. Reason and conscience are God's most precious gifts; and what does He ask but that we make use of them?

Right thinking, like right doing, is the result of innumerable efforts, innumerable failures, the final outcome of which is a habit of right thought and conduct.

Whoever believes in truth, freedom, and love, and follows after them with his whole heart, walks in God's highway, which leads to peace and blessedness.

A thing may be obscure from defect of light or defect of sight; and in the same way an author may be found dull either because he is so, or because his readers are dull. The noblest book even is but dead matter until a mind akin to its creator's awakens it to life again.

The appeal to the imagination has infinitely more charm than the appeal to the senses.

"But when evening falls," says Machiavelli, "I go home and enter my study. On the threshold I lay aside my country garments, soiled with mire, and array myself in courtly garb. Thus attired, I make my entrance into the ancient courts of the men of old, where they receive me with love, and where I feed upon that food which only is my own, and for which I was born. For four hours' space I feel no annoyance, forget all care; poverty cannot frighten nor death appall me." A man of genius works for all, for he compels all to think. An enlightened mind and a generous heart make the world good and fair.

Where there is perfect confidence, conversation does not drag; while for those who love it is enough that they be together: if they are silent, it is well; if they speak, mere nothings suffice.

The world of knowledge, all that men know, is, in truth, little and simple enough. It seems vast and intricate because we are imperfectly educated.

The soul, like the body, has its atmosphere, out of which it cannot live.

When opinions take the place of convictions, ideas that of beliefs, great characters become rare.

The pith of virtue lies not in thinking, but in doing. A real man strives to assert himself; for whether he seeks wealth, or power, or fame, or truth, or virtue, or the good of his fellows, he knows that he can succeed only through self-assertion, through the prevalence of his own thought and life.

They who abdicate the rights God gives the individual, seek in vain to preserve by constitutional enactments a semblance of liberty.

If it is human to hate whom we have injured, it is not less so to despise whom we have deceived; and yet those who are easily deceived are the most innocent or the most high-minded and generous. It seems hardly a human and must therefore be a divine thing, to live and deal with men without in any way giving them trouble and annoyance. Truth loves not contention, and when men fight for it, it vanishes in the noise and smoke of the combat.

The controversies of the schools, whether of philosophy, theology, literature, or natural science, have been among the saddest exhibitions of ineptitude. Is it conceivable that a thinker, or a believer, or a scholar, or an investigator should wrangle in the spirit of a pothouse politician? The more certain we are of ourselves and of the truth of what we hold, the easier it is for us to be patient and tolerant.

Wicked is whoever finds pleasure in another's pain. We can know more than we can love. Hence communion with the world is wider through the mind than through the heart, though less intimate and less satisfying. It is, however, longer active, for we continue to be delighted by new truth when we have ceased to care to make new friends. Learn to bear the faults of men as thou sufferest the changes of weather,—with equanimity; for impatience and anger will no more improve thy neighbors than they will prevent its being hot or cold. What men think or say of thee is unimportant—give heed to what thou thyself thinkest and sayst. If thou art ignored or reviled, remember such has been the fate of the best, while the world's favorites are often men of blood or lust or mere time-servers. He who does genuine work is conscious of the worth of what he does, and is not troubled with misgivings or discouraged by lack of recognition. If God looked away from His universe it would cease to be; and He sees him. The more we detach ourselves from crude realism, from the naive views of uneducated minds, the easier it becomes for us to lead an intellectual and religious life, for such detachment enables us to realize that the material world has meaning and beauty only when it has passed through the alembic of the spirit and become purified, fit object for the contemplation of God and of souls. They are true students who are drawn to seek knowledge by mental curiosity, by affinity with the intelligible, like that which binds and holds lover to lover, making their love all-sufficient and above all price. All that is of value in thy opinions is the truth they contain—to hold them dearer than truth is to be irrational and perverse. Thy faith is what thou believest, not what thou knowest. The crowd loves to hear those who treat the tenets of their opponents with scorn, who overwhelm their adversaries with abuse, who make a mockery of what their foes hold sacred; but to vulgarity of this kind a cultivated mind cannot stoop. To do so is a mark of ignorance and inferiority; is to confuse judgment, to cloud intellect, and to strengthen prejudice. If there are any who are so absurd or so perverse as to be unworthy of fair and rational treatment, to refute them is loss of time, to occupy one's self with them is to keep bad company. With the contentious, who are always dominated by narrow and petty views and motives, enter not into dispute, but look beyond to the wide domain of reason and to the patience and charity of Christ. When minds are alive and active, opposing currents of thought necessarily arise. Contradiction is the salt which keeps truth from corruption. As we let the light fall at different angles upon a precious stone, and change our position from point to point to study a work of art, so it is well to give more than one expression to the same truth, that the intellectual rays falling upon it from several directions, and breaking into new tints and shades, its full meaning and worth may finally be brought clearly into view. If those with whom thou art thrown appear to thee to be hard and narrow, call to mind that they have the same troubles and sorrows as thyself, essentially too the same thoughts and yearnings; and as, in spite of all thy faults, thou still lovest thyself, so love them too, even though they be too warped and prejudiced to appreciate thy worth.

The wise man never utters words of scorn,
For he best knows such words are devil-born.

Our opponents are as necessary to us as our friends, and when those who have nobly combated us die, they seem to take with them part of our mental vigor; they leave us with a deeper sense of the illusiveness of life. Freedom is found only where honest criticism of men and measures is recognized as a common right.

As one man's meat is another's poison, so in the world of intelligible things what refreshes and invigorates one, may weary and depress another. What delights the child makes no impression upon the man. Men and women, the ignorant and the learned, philosophers and poets, mothers and maidens, doers and dreamers, find their entertainment largely in different worlds. Napoleon despised the idealogue; the idealogue sees in him but a conscienceless force.

Outcries against wrong have little efficacy. They alone improve men who inspire them with new confidence, new courage, who help them to renew and purify the inner sources of life. Harsh zeal provokes excess, because it provokes contradiction. Whoever stirs the soul to new depths, whoever awakens the mind to new thoughts and aspirations, is a benefactor. The common man sees the fruits of his toil; the seed which divine men sow, ripens for others. The counsels worldlings give to genius can only mislead. Not only the truth which Christ taught, but the truth which nearly all sublime thinkers have taught, has seemed to the generation to which it was announced but a beggarly lie. The powerful have sneered with Pilate, while the mob have done the teachers to death.

Make truth thy garb, thy house, wherein thou movest and dwellest, and art comfortable and at home.

If thou knowest what thou knowest and believest what thou believest, thou canst not be disturbed by contradiction, but shalt feel that thy opposers are appointed by God to confirm thee in truth.

As the merchant keeps journal and ledger, so should he whose wealth is truth, take account in writing of the thoughts he gains from observation, reflection, reading, and intercourse with men. We become perfectly conscious of our impressions only in giving expression to them; hence ability to express what we feel and know is one of the chief and most important aims and ends of education.

What thou mayst not learn without employing spies, or listening to the stories of the malignant or the gossip of the vulgar, be content not to know.

Our miseries spring from idleness and sin; and idleness is sin and the mother of sin. "To confide in one's self and become something of worth," says Michelangelo, "is the best and safest course." Life-weariness, when it is not the result of long suffering, comes of lack of love, for to love any human being in a true and noble way makes life good. Whatever mistakes thou mayst have made in the choice of a profession and in other things, it is still possible for thee to will and do good, to know truth, and to love beauty, and this is the best life can give. Think of living, and thou shalt find no time to repine.

The character of the believer determines the character of his faith, whatever the formulas by which it is expressed. What we are is the chief constituent of the world in which we now live, and this must be true also of the world in which we believe and for which we hope. For the sensualist a spiritual heaven has neither significance nor attractiveness. The highest truth the noblest see has no meaning for the multitude, or but a distorted meaning. What is divinest in the teaching of Christ, only one in thousands, now after the lapse of centuries, rightly understands and appreciates. It is not so much the things we believe, know, and do, as the things on which we lay the chief stress of hope and desire, that shape our course and decide our destiny.

They alone receive the higher gifts, who, to obtain them, renounce the lower pleasures and rewards of life. Those races are noblest, those individuals are noblest, who care most for the past and the future, whose thoughts and hopes are least confined to the world of sense which from moment to moment ceaselessly urges its claims to attention. Desire fanned by imagination, when it turns to sensual things, makes men brutish; but when its object is intellectual and moral, it lifts them to worlds of pure and enduring delight.

When we would form an estimate of a man, we consider not what he knows, believes, and does, but what kind of being his knowledge, faith, and works have made of him. He who makes us learn more than he teaches has genius. Whoever has freed himself from envy and bitterness may begin to try to see things as they are.

Each one is the outcome of millions of causes, which, so far as he can see, are accidental. How ridiculous then to complain that if this or that only had not happened, all would be well. It is ignorance or prejudice to make a man's conduct an argument against the worth of his writings. Byron was a bad man, but a great poet; Bacon was venal, but a marvellous thinker.

Books, to be interesting to the many, must abound in narrative, must run on like chattering girls, and make little demand upon attention. The appeal to thought is like a beggar's appeal for alms,—heeded by one only in hundreds who pass; for, to the multitude, mental effort is as disagreeable as parting with their money.

A newspaper is old the day after its publication, and there are many books which issue from the press withered and senile, but the best, like the gods, are forever young and delightful.

"Whatever bit of a wise man's work," says Ruskin, "is honestly and benevolently done, that bit is his book or his piece of art. It is mixed always with evil fragments,—ill-done, redundant, affected work; but if you read rightly, you will easily discover the true bits, and *those* are the book." Again: "No book is worth anything which is not worth much; nor is it serviceable until it has been read and re-read, and loved, and loved again; and marked so that you may refer to the passages you want in it."

Unity, steadfastness, and power of will mark the great workers. A dominant impulse urges them forward, and with firm tread they move on till death bids them stay. As the will succumbs to idleness and sin, it can be developed and maintained in health and vigor only by right action.

If thou makest thy intellectual and moral improvement thy chief business, thou shalt not lack for employment, and with thy progress thy joy and freedom shall increase.

Progress is betterment of life. The accumulation of discoveries, the multiplication of inventions, the improvement of the means of comfort, the extension of instruction, and the perfecting of methods, are valuable in the degree in which they contribute to this end. The characteristic of progress is increase of spiritual force. In material progress even, the intellectual and moral element is the value-giving factor. Progress begets belief in progress. As we grow in worth and wisdom, our faith in knowledge and conduct is developed and confirmed, and with more willing hearts we make ourselves the servants of righteousness and love; for in the degree in which religion and culture prevail within us, co-operation for life tends to supersede the struggle for life, which if not the dominant law, is, at least, the general course of things when left to Nature's sway.

Catchwords, such as progress, culture, enlightenment, and liberty, are for the multitude rarely more than psittacisms, mere parrot sounds. So long as we genuinely believe in an ideal and strive to incarnate it, the spirit of hope kindles the flame of enthusiasm within the breast. Its attainment, however, if the ideal is sensual or material, leads to disappointment and weariness. Behold yonder worshipper at the shrine of money and pleasure, whose life is but a yawn between his woman and his wine. But if the ideal is spiritual, failure in the pursuit cannot dishearten us, and success but opens to view diviner worlds towards which we turn our thought and love with self-renewing freshness of mind.

If thou seekest for beauty, it is everywhere; if for hideousness, it too is everywhere.

To believe in one's self, to have genuine faith in the impressions, thoughts, hopes, loves, and aspirations which are in one's own soul, and to strive ceaselessly to come to clear knowledge of this inner world which each one bears within himself, is the secret of culture. To bend one's will day by day to the weaving this light of the mind and warmth of the heart into the substance of life, into conduct, is the secret of character. At whatever point of time or space we find ourselves, we can begin or continue the task of self-improvement; for the only essential thing is the activity of the soul, seeking to become conscious of itself, through and in God and His universe.

> The little bird upbuilds its nest
> Of little things by ceaseless quest:
> And he who labors without rest
> By little steps will reach life's crest.

The true reader is brought into contact with a personality which reveals itself or permits its secret to be divined. In spirit and imagination he lives the life of the author. In his book he finds the experience and wisdom of years compressed into a few pages which he reads in an hour. The vital sublimation of what made a man is thus given him in its essence to exalt or to degrade, to inspire or to deaden his soul. In looking through the eyes of another, he learns to see himself, to understand his affinities and his tendencies, his strength and his weakness. Eat this volume and go speak to the children of Israel, said the spirit to the prophet Ezekiel. The meaning is—mentally devour, digest, and assimilate the book into the fibre and structure of thy very being, and then shalt thou be able to utter words of truth and wisdom to God's chosen ones. The world's spiritual wealth, so far as it has existence other than in the minds of individuals, is stored in literature, in books,—the great treasure-house of the soul's life, of what the best and greatest have thought, known, believed, felt, suffered, desired, toiled, and died for; and whoever fails to make himself a home in this realm of truth, light, and freedom, is shut out from what is highest and most divine in human experience, and sinks into the grave without having lived.

To those who have uttered themselves in public speech, there comes at times a feeling akin to self-reproach. They have taken upon themselves the office of teacher, and yet what have they taught that is worth knowing and loving? They have lost the privacy in which so much of the charm and freedom of life consists; they have been praised or blamed without discernment; and a great part of what they have said and written seems to themselves little more than a skeleton from which the living vesture has fallen. Ask them not to encourage any one to become an author. The more they have deafened the world with their voices, the more will they, like Carlyle, praise the Eternal Silence. They have in fact been taught, by hard experience, that the worth of life lies not in saying or writing anything whatever, but in pure faith, in humble obedience, in brave and steadfast striving. The woman who sweeps a room, the mother who nurses her child, the laborer who sows and reaps, believing and feeling that they are working with God, are leading nobler lives and doing diviner things than the declaimers and theorizers, and the religion which upholds them and lightens their burdens is better than all the philosophies.

Chapter III.

The Making of One's Self.

> The wise man will esteem above everything and will cultivate those sciences which further the perfection of his soul.—PLATO.

It has become customary to call these endings of the scholastic year commencements; just as the people of the civilized world have agreed to make themselves absurd by calling the ninth month the seventh, the tenth the eighth, the eleventh the ninth, and the twelfth the tenth. And, indeed, the discourses which are delivered on these occasions would be more appropriate and more effective if made to students who, having returned from the vacations with renewed physical vigor, feel also fresh urgency to exercise of mind. But now, so little is man in love with truth, the approach of the moment when you are to make escape and find yourselves in what you imagine to be a larger and freer world, occupies all your thoughts, and thrills you with an excitement which makes attention difficult; and, like the noise of crowds and brazen trumpets, prevents the soul from mounting to the serene world where alone it is free and at home.

Since, however, the invitation with which I have been honored directs my address to the graduates of Notre Dame in this her year of Golden Jubilee, I may, without abuse of the phrase, entitle it a commencement oration; for the day on which a graduate worthy of the name leaves his college is the commencement day of a new life of study, more earnest and more effectual than that which is followed within academic walls, because it is the result of his sense of duty alone and of his uncontrolled self-activity. And, though I am familiar with the serious disadvantages with which a reader as compared with a speaker has to contend, I shall read my address, if for no other reason, because I shall thus be able to measure my time; and if I am prolix, I shall be so maliciously, and not become so through the obliviousness which may result from the illusive enthusiasm that is sometimes produced in the speaker by his own vociferation, and which he fondly imagines he communicates to his hearers.

The chief benefit to be derived from the education we receive in colleges and universities, and from the personal contact into which we are there thrown with enlightened minds, is the faith it tends to inspire and confirm in the worth of knowledge and culture, of conduct and religion; for nothing else we there acquire will abide with us as an inner impulse to self-activity, a self-renewing urgency to the pursuit of excellence. If we fail, we fail for lack of faith; but belief is communicated from person to person,—*fides ex auditu*,—and to mediate it is the educator's chief function. Through daily intercourse with one who is learned and wise and noble, the young gain a sense of the reality of science and culture, of religion and morality; which thus cease to be for them vague somethings of which they have heard and read, and become actual things,—realities, like monuments they have inspected, or countries through which they have travelled. They have been taken by the hand and led where, left to themselves, they would never have gone. The true educator inspires not only faith, but admiration also, and confidence and love,—all soul-evolving powers. He is a master whose pupils are disciples,—followers of him and believers in the wisdom he teaches. He founds a school which, if it does not influence the whole course of thought and history, like that of Plato or Aristotle, does at least form a body of men, distinguished by zeal for truth and love of intellectual and moral excellence. To be able thus, in virtue of one's intelligence and character, to turn the generous heart and mind of youth to sympathy with what is intelligible, fair, and good in thought and life, is to be like God,—is to have power in its noblest and most human form; and its exercise is the teacher's chief and great reward. To be a permanent educational force is the highest earthly distinction. Is not this the glory of the founders of religions, of the discoverers of new worlds?

In stooping to the mind and heart of youth, to kindle there the divine flame of truth and love, we ourselves receive new light and warmth. To listen to the noise made by the little feet of children when at play, and to the music of their merry laughter, is pleasant; but to come close to the aspiring soul of youth, and to feel the throbbings of its deep and ardent yearnings for richer and wider life, is to have our faith in the good of living revived and intensified. It is the divine privilege of the young to be able to believe that the world can be moulded and controlled by thought and spiritual motives; and in breathing this celestial air, the choice natures among them learn to become sages and saints; or if it be their lot to be thrown into the fierce struggles where selfish and cruel passions contend for the mastery over justice and humanity, they carry into the combat the serene strength of reason and conscience; for their habitual and real home is in the unseen world, where what is true and good has the Omnipotent for its defence. Of this soul of youth we may affirm without fear of error—

> "The soul seeks God; from sphere to sphere it moves,
> Immortal pilgrim of the Infinite."

Life is the unfolding of a mysterious power, which in man rises to self-consciousness, and through self-consciousness to the knowledge of a world of truth and order and love, where action may no longer be left wholly to the sway of matter or to the impulse of instinct, but may and should be controlled by reason and conscience. To further this process by deliberate and intelligent effort is to educate. Hence education is man's conscious co-operation with the Infinite Being in promoting the development of life; it is the bringing of life in its highest form to bear upon life, individual and social, that it may raise it to greater perfection, to ever-increasing potency. To educate, then, is to work with the Power who makes progress a law of living things, becoming more and more active and manifest as we ascend in the scale of being. The motive from which education springs is belief in the goodness of life and the consequent desire for richer, freer, and higher life. It is the point of union of all man's various and manifold activity; for whether he seeks to nourish and preserve his life, or to prolong and perpetuate it in his descendants, or to enrich and widen it in domestic and civil society, or to grow more conscious of it through science and art, or to strike its roots into the eternal world through faith and love, or in whatever other way he may exert himself, the end and aim of his aspiring and striving is educational,—is the unfolding and uplifting of his being.

The radical craving is for life,—for the power to feel, to think, to love, to enjoy. And as it is impossible to reach a state in which we are not conscious that this power may be increased, we can find happiness only in continuous progress, in ceaseless self-development. This craving for fulness of life is essentially intellectual and moral, and its proper sphere of action is the world of thought and conduct. He who has a healthy appetite does not long for greater power to eat and drink. A sensible man who has sufficient wealth for independence and comfort does not wish for more money; but he who thinks and loves and acts in obedience to conscience feels that he is never able to do so well enough, and hence an inner impulse urges him to strive for greater power of life, for perfection. He is akin to all that is intelligible and good, and is drawn to bring himself into ever-increasing harmony with this high world. Hence attention is for him like a second nature, for attention springs from interest; and since he feels an affinity with all things, all things interest him. And what is thus impressed upon his mind and heart he is impelled to utter in deed or speech or gesture or song, or in whatever way thought and sentiment may manifest themselves. Attention and expression are thus the fundamental forms of self-activity, the primary and essential means of education, of developing intellectual and moral power.

Interest is aroused and held by need, which creates desire. If we are hungry, whatever may help us to food interests us. Our first and indispensable interests relate to the things we need for self-preservation and the perpetuation of the race; and to awaken desire and stimulate effort to obtain them, instinct is sufficient, as we may see in the case of mere animals. But as progress is made, higher and more subtle wants are developed. We crave for more than food and wife and children. The social organism evolves itself; and as its complexity increases, the relations of the individual to the body of which he is a member are multiplied, and become more intricate. As we pass from the savage to the barbarous, and from the barbarous to the civilized state, intellect and conscience are brought more and more into play. Mental power gains the mastery over brute force, and little by little subdues the energies of inorganic nature, and makes them serve human ends. Iron is forced to become soft and malleable, and to assume every shape; the winds bear man across the seas; the sweet and gentle water is imprisoned and tortured until with its fierce breath it does work in comparison with which the mythical exploits of gods and demi-gods are as the play of children. Strength of mind and character takes precedence of strength of body. Hercules and Samson are but helpless infants in the presence of the thinker who reads Nature's secret and can compel her to do his bidding. If we bend our thoughts to this subject, we shall gain insight into the meaning and purpose of education, which is nothing else than the urging of intellect and conscience to the conquest of the world, and to the clear perception and practical acknowledgment of the primal and fundamental truth that man is man in virtue of his thought and love.

Instruction, which is but part of education, has for its object the development of the intellect and the transmission of knowledge. This, whether we consider the individual or society, is indispensable. It is good to know. Knowledge is not only the source of many of our highest and purest joys, but without it we can attain neither moral nor material good in the nobler forms. Virtue when it is enlightened gains a higher quality. And if we hold that action and not thought is the end of life, we cannot deny that action is, in some degree at least, controlled and modified by thought. Nevertheless, instruction is not the principal part of education; for human worth is more essentially and more intimately identified with character and heart than with knowledge and intellect. What we will is more important than what we know; and the importance of what we know is derived largely from its influence on the will or conduct.

A nation, like an individual, receives rank from character more than from knowledge; since the true measure of human worth is moral rather than intellectual. The teaching of the school becomes a subject of passionate interest, through our belief in its power to educate sentiment, stimulate will, and mould character. For in the school we do more than learn the lessons given us: we live in an intellectual and moral atmosphere, acquire habits of thought and behavior; and this, rather than what we learn, is the important thing. To imagine that youths who have passed through colleges and universities, and have acquired a certain knowledge of languages and sciences, but have not formed strongly marked characters, should forge to the front in the world and become leaders in the army of religion and civilization, is to cherish a delusion. The man comes first; and scholarship without manhood will be found to be ineffectual. The semi-culture of the intellect, which is all a mere graduate can lay claim to, will but help to lead astray those who lack the strength of moral purpose; and they whom experience has made wise expect little from young men who have bright minds and have passed brilliant examinations, but who go out into the world without having trained themselves to habits of patient industry and tireless self-activity.

Man is essentially a moral being; and he who fails to become so, fails to become truly human. Individuals and nations are brought to ruin not by lack of knowledge, but by lack of conduct. "Now that the world is filled with learned men," said Seneca, "good men are wanting." He was Nero's preceptor, and saw plainly how powerless intellectual culture was to save Rome from the degeneracy which undermined its civilization and finally brought on its downfall. If in college the youth does not learn to govern and control himself,—to obey and do right in all things, not because he has not the power to disobey and do wrong, but because he has not the will,—nothing else he may learn will be of great service. It seems to me I perceive in our young men a lack of moral purpose, of sturdiness, of downright obstinate earnestness, in everything—except perhaps in money-getting pursuits; for even in these they are tempted to trust to speculation and cunning devices rather than to persistent work and honesty, which become a man more than crowns and all the gifts of fortune. Without truthfulness, honesty, honor, fidelity, courage, integrity, reverence, purity, and self-respect no worthy or noble life can be led. And unless we can get into our colleges youths who can be made to drink into their inmost being this vital truth, little good can be accomplished there. Now, it often happens that these institutions are, in no small measure, refuges into which the badly organized families of the wealthy send their sons in the vain expectation that the fatal faults of inheritance and domestic training will be repaired. In college, as wherever there are men, quality is more precious than quantity. The number of students is great enough when they are of the right kind; and the work which now lies at our hand is to make it possible that those who have talent and the will to improve themselves may enter our institutions of learning. But those who are shown to be insusceptible of education should be eliminated; for they profit not themselves, and are a hindrance to the others.

Gladly I turn from them to you, young gentlemen, who have persevered in the pursuit of knowledge and virtue, and to-day are declared worthy to receive the highest honor Notre Dame can confer. The deepest and the best thing in us is faith in reason; for when we look closely, we perceive that faith in God, in the soul, in good, in freedom, in truth, is faith in reason. Individuals, nations, the whole race, wander in a maze of errors. The world of the senses is apparent and illusive, that of pure thought vague and shadowy. Science touches but the form and surface; speculation is swallowed in abysses and disperses itself; ignorance darkens, passion blinds the mind; the truth of one age becomes the error of a succeeding; opinions change from continent to continent and from century to century. The more we learn, the less we know; and what we most of all desire to know eludes our grasp. But, nevertheless, our faith in reason is unshaken; and holding to this faith, we hold to God, to good, to freedom, and to truth.

Goodness is the radical principle; the good, the primal aim and final end of life; for the good is whatever is helpful to life. Hence what is true is good, what is useful is good, what is fair is good, what is right is good; and the true, the useful, the fair, and the right are intertwined and circle about man like a noble sisterhood, to waken him to life, and to urge him toward God, the supreme good, whose being is power, wisdom, love without limit. The degree of goodness in all things is measured by their approach to this absolute Being. Hence the greater our strength, wisdom, and love, the greater our good, the richer and more perfect our life. There is no soul which does not bow with delight and reverence before Beauty and Power; and when we come to true insight, we perceive that holiness is Beauty and goodness Power. Genuine spiritual power is from God, and compels the whole mechanic world to acknowledge its absoluteness. The truths of religion and morality are of the essence of our life; they cannot be learned from another, but must be wrought into self-consciousness by our own thinking and doing,—by habitual meditation, and constant obedience to conscience. Virtue, knowledge, goodness, and greatness are their own reward: they are primarily and essentially ends, and only incidentally means. Hence those who strive for perfection with the view thereby to gain recognition, money, or place, do not really strive for perfection at all. They are also unwise; for virtue, knowledge, goodness, and greatness are not the surest means to such ends, and they can be acquired only with infinite pains. The highest human qualities cease to be the highest when they are made subordinate to the externalities of office and wealth. The one aim of a mind smitten with the love of excellence is to live consciously and lovingly with whatever is true or good or fair. And such a one cannot be disturbed whether by the general indifference of men or by their praise or blame. The standpoint of the soul is: What thou art, not what others think thee. If thou art at one with thy true self, God and the eternal laws bear thee up and onward. The moral and the religious life interpenetrate each other. To sunder them is to enfeeble both. To weaken faith is to undermine character; to fail in conduct is to deprive faith of inspiration and vigor. Learn to live thy religion, and thou shalt have little need or desire to argue and dispute about it. Truth is mightier than its witnesses, religion greater than its saints and martyrs. Learn to think, and thou shalt easily learn to live.

In the presence of the highest manifestations of thought and love, of truth and beauty, nothing perfect or divine is incredible. Men of genius, philosophers, poets, and saints, who by thinking and doing make this ethereal but most real world rise before us in concrete form and substance, are heavenly messengers and illuminators of the soul. Had none of them lived, how should we see and understand that man is Godlike and that God is truth and love? We cannot make this high world plain by telling about it. It is not a land which may be described. It is a state of soul which they alone comprehend who have been transformed by patient meditation and faithful striving. But once it is revealed, a thousand errors and obscurities fall away from us. If not educated, strive at least to be educable,—a believer in wisdom, and sensitive to all high influence, and eager to be quit of thy ignorance and hardness. As the dead cannot produce the live, so mechanical minds, however much they may be able to drill, train, and instruct, cannot educate. The secret of the mother's specific educational power lies in the fact that she is a spiritual not a mechanical force, loves and is loved by her pupils. The most ennobling and the most thoroughly satisfying sentiment of which we are capable is love. Until we love we are strangers to ourselves. We are like beings asleep or lost to the knowledge of themselves and all things, till, awakening to the appeal of the pure light and the balmy air, they look upon what is not themselves; and, finding it fair and beautiful, learn in loving it to feel and know themselves.

Increase of the power to love is increase of life. But love needs guidance. We first awaken in the world of the senses, and are attracted by what we see and touch and taste. The aim of education is to help the soul to rise above this world, in which, if we remain, we are little better than brutes. Hence the teacher seeks in many ways to reveal to the young the fact that the perfect, the best, cannot be seen or touched, cannot be grasped even by the mind; but that it is, nevertheless, that which they should strive to make themselves capable of loving above all things. And thus he prepares them to understand what is meant by the love of truth and righteousness, by the love of God. In the training of animals even, patience and gentleness are more effective than violence. How, then, shall we hope by physical constraint and harsh methods to educate human beings, who are human precisely because they are capable of love and are swayed by rational motives? There is no soul so gross, so deeply buried in matter, but it shall from some point or other make a sally to show it still bears the impress of God's image. At such points the educator will keep watch, studying how he may make this single ray of light interfuse itself with his pupil's whole being.

It is not possible to know there is no God, no soul, no free will, no right or wrong; at the worst, it is only possible to doubt all this. The universe is as inconceivable as God, and theories of matter as full of difficulties as theories of spirit. It is a question of belief or unbelief; ultimately a question of health or disease, of life or death. They who have no faith in God can have little faith in the worth of life, which can be for them but an efflorescence of death, a sort of inexplicable malady of atoms dreaming they are conscious. If the age tends irresistibly to destroy belief in God, the end will be the ruin of belief in the good of life. In the mean while the doubt which weakens the springs of hope and love is not a symptom of health but of disease, pregnant with suffering and misery for all, but most of all for the young. He who is loved in a true and noble way is surrounded by an element of spiritual light in which his worth is revealed to him. In perceiving what he is to another, he comes to understand what he is or may be in himself.

Our self respect even is largely due to the love we receive in childhood and youth. Enthusiasm springs from faith in God and in the soul, which begets in us a high and heroic belief in the divine good of life. It is thus an educational force of highest value. It calms and exalts the soul like the view of the starlit heavens and the everlasting mountains. It is, in every good and noble cause, a fountain head of endurance and perseverance. It bears us on with a sense of joy and vigor, such as is felt when, mounted on a high-mettled steed, we ride in the pleasant air of a spring morning, amid the beauties and grandeurs of nature. In the front of battle and in the presence of death it throws around the soul the light of immortal things. It gives us the plenitude of existence, the full and high enjoyment of living. On its wings the poet, the lover, the orator, the hero, and the saint are borne in rapture through worlds whose celestial glory and delightfulness cold and unmoved minds do not suspect. It is not a flame from the dry wood and withered grass, but a heat and glow from the abysmal depths of being. It makes us content to follow after truth and love in dark and narrow ways, as the miner, in central deeps where sunlight has never fallen, seeks his treasure. It keeps us fresh and young; and, like the warmer sun, reclothes the world day by day with new beauty. It teaches patience, the love of work without haste and without worry. It gives strength to hear and speak truth, and to walk in the sacred way of truth, as though we but idly strolled with pleasant friends amid fragrant flowers. It gives us deeper consciousness of our own liberty, faith in human perfectibility, which lies at the root of our noblest efforts; to which the more we yield ourselves the more we feel that we are free. It knows a thousand words of truth and might, which it whispers in gentlest tones to rightly attuned ears: Since the universe is a harmony whose diapason is God, why should thy life strike a discordant note? Yield not to discouragement; thou art alive, and God is in His world. The combat and not the victory proclaims the hero. If thy success had been greater, thou hadst been less. The noisy participants in great conflicts, of whatever kind, exercise less influence upon the outcome than choice spirits, who, turning aside from the thunder and smoke of battle, gain in lonely striving and meditation view of new truth by which the world is transformed.

We owe more to Columbus than to Isabella; to Descartes than to Louis XIV.; to Bacon than to Elizabeth; to Pestalozzi than to Napoleon; to Goethe than to Blücher; to Pasteur than to Bismarck. If thou wouldst be persuaded and convinced, persuade and convince thyself. Be thy aim not increase of happiness, but of knowledge, wisdom, power, and virtue; and thou shalt, without thinking of it, find thyself also happy. Character is formed by effort, resistance, and patience. If necessity is the mother of invention, suffering is the mother of high moods and great thoughts. Poets have sung to ease their sorrow-burdened or love-tortured hearts; and the travail of souls yearning with ineffable pain for truth has led to the nearest view of God. Wisdom is the child of suffering, as beauty is the child of love. If a truth discourages thee, thou art not yet ripe for it; for thee it is not yet wholly true. Work not like an ox at the plough, but like a setter afield; not because thou must, but because thou takest delight in thy task. Only they have come of age who have learned how to educate themselves. Education, like life, works from within outward: the teacher loosens the soil and removes the obstacles to light and warmth and moisture; but growth comes of the activity of the soul itself.

A new century will not make new men; but if, in truth, it be a new century, it will be made so by the deeper thought and diviner love of men and women. Let the old tell what they have done, the young what they are doing, and fools what they intend to do.

The power to control attention, as a good rider holds his horse to the road and to his gait, is a result of education; and when it is acquired other things become easy.

Let not poverty or misfortune or insult or flattery or success, O seeker after truth and beauty! turn thee from thy divine task and purpose. Pardon every one except thyself, and put thy trust in God and in thyself. "If I buy thee," asked one of a Spartan captive, "and treat thee well, wilt thou be good?"—"I will," he replied, "if thou buy me or not; or if, having bought me, thou treat me ill."

If there be anything of worth in thee, it will make thee strong and contented; it is so good for thee to have it that thou canst easily forget it is unrecognized by others.

If all sufferings, sorrows, and disappointments had been left out of thy life, wouldst thou be more or less than thou art? Less worthy, doubtless, and less wise. In these evils, then, there is something good. If thou couldst but bear this always in mind, thou shouldst be better able to suffer pain, whether of body or soul. There are things thou hast greatly desired which, had they been given thee, would make thee wretched. The wiser thou growest, the better shalt thou understand how little we know what is for the best.

"Had I but lived!" cried Obermann. And a woman of genius replied: "Be consoled, O Obermann! Hadst thou lived, thou hadst lived in vain." So it is. In the end we neither regret that pleasures have been denied us, nor feel that those we have enjoyed were a gain unless they are associated with the memory of high faith and thought and virtuous action. He who is careful to fill his mind with truth and his heart with love will not lack for retreats in which he may take refuge from the stress and storms of life. Noise, popularity, and buncombe: onions, smoke, and bedbugs.

Be thy own rival, comparing thyself with thyself, and striving day by day to be self-surpassed. If thy own little room is well lighted the whole world is less dark. If thou art busy seeking intellectual and moral illumination and strength, thou shalt easily be contented. Higher place would mean for thee less liberty, less opportunity to become thyself. The secret of progress lies in knowing how to make use, not of what we have chosen, but of what is forced upon us. To occupy one's self with trifles weans from the habit of work more effectually than idleness. Perfect skill comes of talent, study, and exercise; and the study and exercise must continue through the whole course of life. To cease to learn is to lose freshness and the power to interest. We lack will rather than strength; are able to do more and better than we are inclined to do; and say we can not because we have not the courage to say we will not. The law of unstable equilibrium applies to thee, as to whatever has life. Thou canst not remain what thou art, but must rise or fall. The body is under the sway of physical law, but the progress of the mind is left in a large measure to the play of free will. If thou willest what thou oughtest, thou canst do what thou willest; for obligation cannot transcend ability. Happy are they who from earliest youth understand the meaning of duty, and hearken to the stern but all-reasonable voice of this daughter of God, the smile upon whose face is the fairest thing we know.

He who willingly accepts the law of moral necessity is free; for in thus accepting it he transcends it, and is self-determined; while he who rebels against this law sinks to a lower plane of being than the properly human, and becomes the slave of appetite and passion. Duty means sacrifice; it is a turning from the animal to the spiritual self; from the allurements of the world of manifold sensation—from ease, idleness, gain, and pleasure—to the high and lonely regions, where the command of conscience speaks in the name of God and of the nature of things. Forget thyself and do thy best, as unconscious of vain-glorious thoughts as though thou wert a wind or a stream, an impersonal force in the service of God and man. Obey conscience, and laugh in the face of death. Convince thyself that the best thing for thee is to know truth and to make truth the law of thy life. Let this faith subordinate all else, as it is, indeed, faith in reason and in God. Abhorrence of lies is the test of character. Hold fast by what thou knowest to be true, not doubting for a moment because thou canst not reconcile it with other truth. Somewhere, somehow, truth will be matched with truth, as love mates heart with heart.

A man's word is himself, his reason, his conscience, his faith, his love, his aspiration. If it is false or vain or vile, he is so. It is the expression of life as it has come to consciousness within him. It is the revelation of quality of being; it is of the man himself, his sign and symbol, the form and mould and mirror of his soul.

> Thou thinkest to serve God with lies,
> Thou devil-worshipper and fool!

The moral value of the study of science lies in the love of truth it inspires and inculcates. He who knows science knows that liars are imbeciles. From the educator's point of view, truthfulness is the essential thing. His aim and end is to teach truth, and the love of truth, which leavens the whole mass and makes it life-giving. But the liar has no proper virtue of any kind.

The doubt of an earnest, thoughtful, patient, and laborious mind is worthy of respect. In such doubt there may be found indeed more faith than in half the creeds. But the scepticism of sciolists lacks the depth and genuineness of truth. To be frivolous where there is question of all that gives life meaning and value is want of sense. The sciolist is one who has a superficial knowledge of various things, which for lack of deep views and coherent thought, for lack of the understanding of the principles of knowledge itself, he is unable to bring into organic unity. The things he knows are confused and intermingled, and thus fail either to enlighten his mind or to impel him to healthful activity. He forms opinions lightly and pronounces judgment rashly. Knowing nothing thoroughly, he has no suspicion of the infinite complexity of the world of life and thought. The evil effects of this semi-culture are most disagreeable and most harmful in those whose being has been developed only on its temporal and earthly side. Their spiritual and moral nature has no centre about which it may move, and they wander on the surface of things in self-satisfied conceit, proclaiming that what is beyond the senses is beyond the reach of the mind, as though our innermost consciousness were not of what is intangible and invisible.

All divine things are within and about us, here and now; but we are too gross to see the celestial light, or to catch the whisperings of the heavenly voices. God is here; but we, like plants and mollusks, live in worlds of which we do not dream, upheld and nourished and borne onward by a Power of whom we are but dimly conscious,—nay, of whom, for the most part, we are unconscious.

There is a truth above the reach of logic, an impulse of the mind and heart which urges beyond the realms of sense, beyond the ken of the dialectician, to the Infinite and Eternal, before whom the material universe is but a force at whose finest touch souls awaken to the thrill of thought and love.

When we are made conscious of the fact that the Divine Word is the light of men, we readily understand that our every true thought, our every good deed, our every deeper view of nature and of life, comes from God, who is always urging us into the glorious liberty of His children, until we become a heavenly republic in which righteousness, peace, and joy shall reign. "The restless desire of every man to improve his position in the world is the motive power of all social development, of all progress," says Scherr, unable to perceive that the mightiest impulses to nobler and wider life have been given by those who were not thinking at all of improving their position, but were wholly bent upon improving themselves. Make choice, O youth! between having and being. If having is thy aim, consent to be inferior; if being is thy aim, be content with having little. Real students, cultivators of themselves, are not inspired by the love of fame or wealth or position, but they are driven by an inner impulse to which they cannot but yield. Their enthusiasm is not a fire that blazes for an hour and then dies out; it is a heat from central depths of life, self-fed and inextinguishable.

The impulse to nobler and freer life springs, never from masses of men, but always from single luminous minds and glowing hearts. The lightning of great thoughts shows the way to heroic deeds. It is better to know than to be known, to love than to be loved, to help than to be helped; for since life is action, it is better to act than to be acted upon. Whosoever makes himself purer, worthier, wiser, works for his country, works for God. The belief that the might of truth is so great that it must prevail in spite of whatever opposition, needs, to say the least, interpretation; for it has often happened that truth has been overcome for whole generations and races; and the important consideration is not whether it shall finally prevail, but whether it shall prevail for us, for our own age and people. It is of the nature of spiritual gifts to work in every direction; they enrich the individual and the nation; they develop, purify, and refine the intellectual, moral, and physical worlds in which men live and strive. The State and the Church are organisms; the body, the social and religious soul, under the guidance of God, creates for itself. And not only should there be no conflict between them, but there should be none between them and the free and full development of the individual. A peasant whose mental state is what it might have been a thousand years ago is for us, however moral and religious, an altogether unsatisfactory kind of man. All knowledge is pure, and all speech is so if it spring from the simple desire to utter what is seen and recognized as truth. The love of liberty is rare. It is not found in those whose life-aim is money, pleasure, and place, which enslave; but in those who love truth, which is the only liberating power. Knowledge is the correlative of being, and only a high and loving soul can know what truth is or understand what Christ meant when He said: "Ye shall know truth, and truth shall make you free." High thinking and right loving may make enemies of those around us, but they make us Godlike. How seldom in our daily experience of men do we find one who wishes to be enlightened, reformed, and made virtuous! How easy it is to find those who wish to be pleased and flattered!

At no period in history has civilization been so widespread or so complex as to-day. Never have the organs of the social body been so perfect. Never has it been possible for so many to co-operate intelligently in the work of progress. You, gentlemen, have youth and faith and the elements of intellectual and moral culture. In the freshness and vigor of early manhood, you stand upon the threshold of the new century. You speak Shakspeare's and Milton's tongue; in your veins is the blood which in other lands and centuries has nourished the spirit which makes martyrs, heroes, and saints. Your religion strikes its roots into the historic past of man's noblest achievements, and looks to the future with the serene confidence with which it looks to God. Your country, if not old, is not without glory. Its soil is as fertile, its climate as salubrious as its domain is vast. It is peopled by that Aryan race, which, from most ancient days, has been the creator and invincible defender of art and science and philosophy and liberty; and with all this the divine spirit and doctrine of the Son of Man have been interfused.

We are here in America constituted on the wide basis of universal freedom, universal opportunity, universal intelligence, universal good-will. Our government is the rule of all for the welfare of all; it has stood the test of civil war, and in many ways proved itself both beneficent and strong. Already we have subdued this continent to the service of man. Within a hundred years we have grown to be one of the most populous and wealthy and also one of the most civilized and progressive nations of the earth. Your opportunities are equal to the fullest measure of human worth and genius. In the midst of a high and noble environment it were doubly a disgrace to be low and base. In intellectual and moral processes and results the important consideration is not how much, but what and how. How much, for instance, one has read or written gives us little insight into his worth and character; but when we know what and how he has read and written, we know something of his life. When I am told that America has more schools, churches, and newspapers than any other land, I think of their kind, and am tempted to doubt whether it were not better if we had fewer.

The more general and the higher the average education of the people, the more urgent is the need of thoroughly cultivated and enlightened minds to lead them wisely. The standard of our intellectual and professional education is still low; and neither from the press nor the pulpit nor legislative halls do we hear highest wisdom rightly uttered. To be an intellectual force in this age one must know—must know much and know thoroughly; for now in many places there are a few, at least, who are acquainted with the whole history of thought and discovery, who are familiar with the best thinking of the noblest minds that have ever lived; and to imagine that a sciolist, a half-educated person, can have anything new or important to impart is to delude one's self.

But if you fail, you will fail like all who fail,—not from lack of knowledge, but from lack of conduct; for the burden which in the end bears us down is that of our moral delinquencies. All else we may endure, but that is a sinking and giving way of the source of life itself. It is better, in every way, that you should be true Christian men than that you should do deeds which will make your names famous. And if you could believe this with all your heart, you would find peace and freedom of spirit, even though your labors should seem vain and your lives of little moment. The more reason and conscience are brought to bear upon you, the more will you be lifted into the high and abiding world, where truth and love and holiness are recognized to be man's proper and imperishable good. Become all it is possible for you to become. What this is you can know only by striving day by day, from youth to age, even unto the end; leaving the issue with God and His master-workman, Time.

Chapter IV.

Woman and Education.

> Progress, man's distinctive mark alone;
> Not God's and not the beasts'; God is, they are;
> Man partly is and wholly hopes to be.—*Browning*.

The partialness of man's life, the low level on which the race has been content to dwell, is attributable, in no small measure, to the injustice done to woman. It was assumed she was inferior, and to make the assumption true, she was kept in ignorance, dwarfed and treated as a means rather than as an end.

The right to grow is the primal right; it is the right to live, to unfold our being on every side in the ceaseless striving for truth and love and beauty. In comparison with this, purely political and civil rights are unimportant. And in a free state this fundamental right must not only be acknowledged and defended, but a public opinion must be created which shall declare it to be the most sacred and inviolable. The principle is universal, and is as applicable to woman as to man.

There is not a religion, a philosophy, a science, an art for man and another for woman. Consequently there is not, in its essential elements at least, an education for man and another for woman. In souls, in minds, in consciences, in hearts, there is no sex. What is the best education for woman? That which will best help her to become a perfect human being, wise, loving, and strong. What is her work? Whatever may help her to become herself. What is forbidden her? Nothing but what degrades or narrows or warps. What has she the right to do? Any good and beautiful and useful thing she is able to do without hurt to her dignity and worth as a human being.

Between her and man the real question is not of more and less, of inferiority and superiority, but of unlikeness. Chastity is woman's great virtue; truthfulness, which is the highest form of courage, is man's; yet men and women are equally bound to be chaste and truthful. Mildness and sweet reasonableness are woman's subtlest charms; wisdom and valor, man's; yet women should be wise and brave, and men should be mild and reasonable. The spiritual endowment of the sexes is much the same, but they are not equally interested in the same things. Man prefers thought; woman, sentiment; he reaches his conclusions through analysis and argument; she, through feeling and intuition. He has greater power of self-control; she, of self-sacrifice. He is guided by law and principle; she, by insight and tact; he demands justice; she, equity. He wishes to be honored for wealth and position; she, for herself. For him what he possesses is a means; for her, something to which she holds and is attached. He asks for power; she, for affection. He derives his idea of duty from reason; she, from faith and love. He prefers science and philosophy; she, literature and art. His religion is a code of morality; hers, faith and hope and love and imagination. For her, things easily become persons; for him, persons are little more than things. She has greater power of self-effacement, forgetting herself wholly in her love. Whether she marry or become a nun, she abandons her name, the symbol of her identity, in proof that she is dedicate to the race and to God. The arguments of infidels have less weight with her than with man, for her sense of religion is more genuine, her faith more inevitable. She passes over objections as a chaste mind passes over what is coarse or impure. She more easily finds complacency in her appearance and surroundings, but she has less pride and conceit than man. She is more grateful, too, because she loves more, and the heart makes memory true. If her greater fondness for jewelry and showy adornment proves her to be more barbarous, her greater refinement and chastity prove her to be more civilized than man. And does not her delight in dress come of her care for beauty, which in a world of coarse and ugly creatures is a virtue as fair as the face of spring? Why should the flowers and the fields, the hills and the heavens, be beautiful, and man hideous, and the cities where he abides dismal? Are we but cattle to be stalled and fed? Are corn and beef and iron the only good and useful things? Are we not human because we think and admire, and are exalted in the presence of what is infinitely true and divinely fair?

Faith, hope, and love are larger and more enduring powers for woman than for man. She feeds the sacred fire which never dies on the altars of home and religion and country. She lives a more interior life, and more easily retains consciousness of the soul's reality and of God's presence. If she speaks less of patriotism in peaceful times, in the hour of danger the white light flashes from her soul. It is this that makes brave men think of their mothers and wives and sisters when they march to battle. They know that those sweet hearts, however keen the pangs they suffer, would rather have them dead than craven. When woman shall grow to the full measure of her endowments, a purer flame will glow upon the hearth, and love of country will be a more genuine passion.

If she gain a wider and more varied interest in life, she will become happier, more willing and more able to help the progress of the race. Like man, she exists for herself and God, and in her relations to others, her duties are not to the home alone, but to the whole social body, religious and civil. Whether man or woman, is a minor thing; to be wise and worthy and loving is all in all. Our deeper consciousness and practical recognition of the equality of the sexes is better evidence that we are becoming Christian and civilized than popular government and all our mechanical devices. We, however, still have prejudices as ridiculous and harmful as that which made it unbecoming in a woman to know anything or in a man of birth to engage in business. If we hold that every human being has the right to do whatever is fair or noble or useful, we must also hold that it is wrong to throw hindrance in the way of the complete education of any human being. We at last, however slowly, are approaching the standpoint of Christ, who, with his divine eye upon the sexless soul, overlooks distinctions of sex, and placing the good of life in knowing and loving, in being and doing, makes it the privilege and duty of all to help all to know and love, to become and do. Is it true? Is it right? These are the immortal questions, springing from what within us is most like God, and they who deal deceitfully with them have no claim upon attention. They are jugglers and liars.

What is developed is not really changed, but made more fully itself, and by giving to woman a truer education, the beauty and charm of her nature will be brought more effectively into play. None of us love "a woman impudent and mannish grown;" but knowledge and culture and strength of mind and heart and body have no tendency to produce such a caricature. Whether there is question of man or woman, the aim and end of education is to bring forth in the individual the divine image of humanity as it exists in the thought of God, as it is revealed in the life of Christ.

> "Yet in the long years liker must they grow;
> The man be more of woman, she more of man:
> He gain in sweetness and in moral height,
> Nor lose the wrestling thews that throw the world;
> She mental breadth, nor fail in childward care;
> More as the double-natured poet each."

The apothegm, man is born to do, woman to endure, no longer commends itself to our judgment. Both are born to do and to endure; and in educating girls, we now understand that it is our business to strengthen them and to stimulate them to self-activity. We strive to give them self-control, sanity, breadth of view, wide sympathies, and an abiding sense of justice. One might, indeed, be tempted to think it were well woman should retain a touch of folly, that she still may be able to believe the man she loves is half divine; but to think so one must be a man, with his genius for self-conceit. To train a girl chiefly with a view to success in society is to pervert, is to hinder from attaining to the power of free, rich, and varied life. It is to neglect education for accomplishments; it is to prefer form to substance, manner to conduct, graceful carriage and dress to thought and love. We degrade her when we consider her as little else than a candidate for matrimony. A man may remain single and become the noblest of his kind, and so may a woman. Marriage is first of all for the race; the individual may stand alone and grow to the full measure of human strength and worth. The popular contempt for single women who have reached a certain age, is but a survival of the contempt for all women which is found among savages and barbarians. In the education of woman, as of man, the end is increase of power,—of the might there is in intelligence and love, of the strength there is in gentleness and sweetness and light, of the vigor there is in health, in the rhythmic pulse and in deep breathing, of the sustaining joy there is in pure affection and in devotion to high purposes. Whether there is question of boys or of girls, the safe way is to strive to make them all it is possible for them to become, putting our trust for the rest in human nature and in God; for talent, like genius, is a divine gift, and to prevent its development is to sin against religion and humanity. For girls as for boys, the aim should be not knowledge, but power; not accomplishments, but faculty. Nine-tenths of what we learn in school is quickly forgotten, and is valueless unless it issue in increase of moral and intellectual strength. "In whatever direction I turn my thoughts," says Schleiermacher, "it seems to me that woman's nature is nobler and her life happier than man's; and if ever I play with an idle wish it is that I might be a woman." Hardly any man, I imagine, would rather be a woman, and many women doubtless would rather be men; and yet there is much in Schleiermacher's thought, if we believe, as the wise do believe, that love is the best, and that they who love most are the highest and, therefore, the happiest, since the noblest mind the best contentment has.

What fountains to the desert are,
What flowers to the fresh young spring,
What heaven's breast is to the star,
That woman's love to earth doth bring.

Whether mid deserts she is found,
Or girt about by happy home,
Where'er she treads is holy ground
Above which rises love's high dome.

Or be she mother called or wife,
Or sister or the soul's twin mate,
She still is each man's best of life,
His crown of joy, his high estate.

What is our Christian faith but the revelation of the supreme and infinite worth of love, as being of the essence of God himself? Is it not easy to believe that to a loving soul in an all-chaste body the unseen world may lie open to view? That Joan of Arc saw heavenly visions and heard whisperings from higher worlds, who can doubt that has considered how her most pure womanly soul redeemed a whole people, and, by them forsaken, from midst fierce flames took its flight to God?

Should women vote? The rule of the people is good only when it is the rule of the good and wise among the people, and of these, women, in great numbers, are part. The leadership of the best comes near to being the leadership of God. But the question of the suffrage for women is grave; it is one on which an enlightened mind will long hold judgment in suspense. Does not political life, as it exists in our democracy, tend to corrupt both voters and office-seekers? Is it not largely a life of cant, pretence, and hypocrisy, of venality, corruption, and selfishness, of lying, abuse, and vulgarity? Do not public men, like public women, sell themselves, though in a different way? Is the professional politician, the professional caucus-manipulator, the professional voter, the type of man we can admire or respect even? The objection so frequently raised, that political life would corrupt women, has, at least, the merit of a certain grim humorousness. Could it by any chance make them as bad as it makes men? To tell them they are the queens of the home, to whom the mingling with plebeians is degrading, is an insult to their intelligence. We have forsworn kings and queens, both in private and in public life, and at home women are, for the most part, drudges. What need is there of a hollow phrase when the appeal to truth is obvious?

> "A servant with this clause
> Makes drudgery divine;
> Who sweeps a room as for thy laws,
> Makes that and the action fine."

Active participation in political life is not a refining, an ennobling, a purifying influence. Is it desirable that the half of the people to which the interests of the home, of the heart, of the religious and moral education of the young are especially committed, should be hurled into the maelstrom of selfish passion and coarse excitement?

The smartness and self-assertiveness of American women are already excessive; they lack repose, serenity, and self-restraint. If they rush into the arena of noisy and vulgar strife, will not the evil be increased? Will not the political woman lose something of the sacred power of the wife and mother? Are not the primal virtues, those which make life good and fair and which are a woman's glory,—are they not humble and quiet and unobtrusive? The suffrage has not emancipated the masses of men, who are still held captive in the chains of poverty and dehumanizing toil.

Do women themselves, those, at least, in whom the woman soul, which draws us on and upward, is most itself, desire that the vote be given them?

But whatever our opinions on the subject may be, let us not lose composure. "If a great change is to be made," says Edmund Burke, "the minds of men will be fitted to it, the general opinions and feelings will draw that way. Every fear, every hope will forward it; and then they who persist in opposing the mighty current will appear rather to resist the decrees of Providence itself than the mere designs of men. They will not be resolute and firm, but perverse and obstinate."

Whether or not woman shall become a politician, there is no doubt that she is becoming a worker in a constantly widening field. The elementary education of the country is already intrusted to her. She is taking her position in the higher institutions of learning. She has gained admission to professional life. In the business world, her competition with man is more and more felt. In literature, in our country at least, her appreciativeness is greater than man's, and her performance not inferior to his. There is a larger number of serious students among women than among men. In the divinely imposed task of self-education, they are fast becoming the chief workers. They are the great readers of books, especially of poetry. The muse was the first school-mistress, and the love of genuine poetry is still the finest educational influence. The vulgar passions and coarse appetites which rob young men of faith in the higher life and of the power to labor perseveringly for ideal ends, have little hold upon the soul of woman. Her betrayers are frivolity and vanity, and a too confiding heart; and the more she is educated the less will she take delight in what is merely external, and the greater will become her ability to bring sentiment under the control of reason and conscience.

There are not two educations, then, one for man, and another for woman, but both alike we bid contend to the uttermost for completeness of life; bid both trust in human educableness, which makes possible the hope of attaining all divine things. True faith in education is ever associated with genuine humility. Only they strive infinitely who feel that their lack is infinite.

The power of education is as many sided and as manifold as life. There is no finest seed or flower or fruit, no most serviceable animal, which has not been brought to perfection by human thought and labor, or which, were this help withdrawn, would not degenerate; and if the highest thought and the most intelligent labor were made to bear ceaselessly upon the improvement of the race of man, we should have a new world.

When we consider all the beauty, knowledge, and love which are within man's reach, how is it possible not to believe that infinitely more and higher lie beyond? Call to mind whatever quality of life, physical, intellectual, or moral, and you will have little difficulty in seeing that it is a result of education. We are born, indeed, with unequal endowments; but strength of limb, ease and swiftness of motion, grace and fluency of speech, modulation of voice, distinctness of articulation, correctness of pronunciation, power of attention, fineness of ear, clearness of vision, control of hand and certainty of touch in drawing, writing, painting, playing upon instruments and operating with the knife, truth and vividness of imagination, force of will, refinement of manner, perfection of taste, skill in argument, purity of desire, rectitude of purpose, power of sympathy and love, together with whatever else goes to the making of a perfect man or woman, are all acquired through educational processes.

Education is the training of a human being with a view to make him all he may become; and hence it is possible to educate one's self in many ways and on many sides.

Refinement, grace, and cleanliness are aims and ends, as truly as are vigor and suppleness of mind and strength and purity of heart. Like sunshine and flowers and the songs of birds, they help to make life pleasant and beautiful. Even the fishes are not clean, but the only clean animal is here and there a man or a woman who has forsworn dirt visible and invisible. We can educate ourselves in every direction, to sleep well even, and neither physicians nor poets have told half the good there is in sleep. The bare thought of it always brings to me the memory of lulling showers, and grazing sheep, and murmuring streams, and bees at work, and the breath of flowers and cooing doves and children lying on the sward, and lazy clouds slumbering in azure skies. It is pleasant as the approach of evening, fresh and fair as the rising sun which sets all the world singing, sacred and pure as babes smiling in their dreams on the breasts of gentle mothers. If thou canst not see the divine worth in nature and in works of genius, it is because thou art what thou art. Can the worm at thy feet recognize thy superiority? The blind and the heedless see nothing, O foolish maid.

What I know and love is of my very being, is, in fact, my knowing and loving self. Quality of knowledge and love determines quality of life, and when I know and love God I am divine. As trees are enrooted in earth, as fishes are immersed in water, and our bodies in air, that they may live, so the soul has its being in God that it may have life, that it may know and love. I become self-conscious only in becoming conscious of what is not myself; and when the not-myself is the Eternal, is God, my self-consciousness is divine. The marvel and the mystery of our being is that self-consciousness should exist at all, not that it should continue to exist forever. But words cannot strengthen or explain or destroy our belief in God, in the immortality of the soul, and in the freedom of the will. The antagonism supposed to exist between scientific facts or theories and religious faith would cease to be recognized as real, were it not for the eagerness with which those who are incapable of profound and comprehensive views, catch up certain shibboleths and hurl them like firebrands upon the combustible imaginations of the unthinking.

To prove, means, in the proper sense of the word, to test, to bring ideas, opinions, and beliefs to the ordeal of reason, of accepted standards of judgment. It is a criticism of the mind and its operations, and hence it may easily happen that to prove is to weaken and unsettle. In what is most vital, in belief in God, immortality, and freedom of the will, in religion and morality, our faith is stronger than any proof that may be brought in its defence; and this is not less true of our faith in the reality of nature and the laws of science; and when this is made plain by criticism, those whose mental grasp is weak or partial, are confused and tempted to doubt. They are not helped, but harmed, and our ceaseless discussions and provings, in press and pulpit, are the source of much of the unrest, religious doubt, and moral weakness of the age. The people need to be taught by those who know and believe, not by those whose skill is chiefly syllogistic and critical. Philosophic speculation is like a vast mountain into which men, generation after generation, have sunk shafts in search of some priceless treasure, and have left in the materials they have thrown out the mark and evidence of failure. But the noblest minds will still be haunted by the infinite mystery which they will seek in vain to explain. Their faith in reason, like that of the vulgar, cannot be shaken, nor can defeat, running through thousands of years, enfeeble their courage or dampen their ardor. Let our increasing insight into Nature's laws fill us with thankfulness and joy. It is good, and makes for good. Let us bow with respect and reverence before the army of patient investigators who bring highly disciplined faculties to bear upon the most useful researches. Let knowledge grow. A nearer and truer view of the boundless fact will not make the world less wonderful, or the soul less divine, or God less adorable. If one should declare that it is contrary to the teachings of faith to hold that conversation may be carried on by persons a thousand miles apart, it would be sufficient to reply that such conversation takes place, and that to attempt to annul fact by doctrine is absurd. There is no excuse for the controversial conflict between science and religion; for science is ascertained fact, not theory about fact, and when fact is rightly ascertained it is accepted of all men. The most certain fact, for each one, is that he knows and loves, and that this power comes to him through communion with what is higher and deeper and wider than himself,—with God.

There was a time when collisions among the masses of the sidereal system were frequent, shocks of unimaginable force by which the celestial bodies were shivered into atoms, so that what now remains is but a survival of worlds which escaped destruction in the chaotic struggle when suns madly rushed on one another and rose in star-dust about the face of God, who was, and is, and shall be, eternal and forever the same. Where there is no thinker, there is no thing. It is in, and through, and with Him that we know ourselves and our environment; and recognize that our particular life is, in its implications, universal and divine. He is the principle of unity which is present in whatever is an object of thought, and which gives the mind the power to co-ordinate the manifold of sensation into the harmony of truth; He is the principle of goodness and beauty, which makes the universe fair, and thrills the heart of man with hope and love. Amid endless change, He alone is permanent, and He is power and wisdom and love, and they only are good and wise and strong who cleave to His eternal and absolute being. But since here and now the real world of matter as distinguished from the apparent is hidden behind the veil of sense, it is vain to hope that the world of eternal life shall be made plain to the pure reason. Religion, like life, is faith, hope, and love, striving and doing, not intellectual intuition and beatific vision. We find it impossible to separate our thought of God from that of infinite goodness and love; but when we look away from our own souls to Nature's pitiless and fatal laws, we realize that this faith in all-embracing and all-conquering love is opposed by seemingly insurmountable difficulties. It is a mystery we believe, not a truth we comprehend. Systems of philosophy, morality, and religion, however cunningly devised, cannot make men philosophers, sages, or saints. This they can become only through the communion which faith, hope, and love have power to establish with the living fountain-head of truth, wisdom, and goodness.

The pursuit of knowledge, like the struggle for wealth and place, ends in disillusion, in the disappointment which results from the contrast between what we hope for and what we attain. The greater the success, the more complete the disenchantment. As the rich and famous best see the unsatisfactoriness of wealth and honor, so they who know much best understand how knowledge avails not, how it is but a cloud-built citadel, whose foundations rest upon the uncertain air, whose walls and turrets lose in substance what they gain in height. When we imagine we know all things, we awake as from a dream to find that we know nothing, that our knowing is but a believing, our science but a faith. We are little children who wander in a father's wide domain, seeing many things and understanding not anything, who imagine we are in a real and abiding world, while in truth we are but passing through the picture-gallery of the senses.

> Faith, Hope, and Love:—these three
> Are life's deep root;
> They reach into infinity,
> Whence life doth shoot.
> But Faith and Hope have not attained
> The Eternal best;
> While Love, sweet Love, the end has gained,—
> In God to rest.

So long as these life-begetting, life-sustaining, and life-developing powers hold mightier sway over the soul of woman than over that of man, so long will woman's heel crush the serpent's head and woman's arms bear salvation to the world. She will not worship the rising sun, or become the idolatress of success, but within her heart will cherish fallen heroes and lost causes and the memory of all the sorrows by which God humanizes the world.

If we consider mankind merely as a phenomenon, the extinction of the race need give us little more concern than the disappearance of Pterodactyls and Ichthyosauri. What repels from such contemplation is not man's physical, but his spiritual being,—that which makes him capable of thought and love, of faith and hope. The universe is anthropomorphized, for whithersoever man looks he sees the reflection of his own countenance. What he calls things are stamped with the impress and likeness of himself, as he himself is an image of the eternal mind, in which all things are mirrored.

An atheist or a materialist, an agnostic or a pessimist, may have greater knowledge, greater intellectual force than the most devout believer in God; but is it possible for him to feel so thoroughly at home in the world, to feel so deeply that, whatever happens, it is and will be well with him? In an atheistic world the spirit of man is ill at ease. He who has no God makes himself the centre of all things, and, like a spoiled child, loses the power to admire, to enjoy, and to love. Genuine faith in God is such an infinite force that one may be tempted to doubt whether it is found.

Undisciplined minds become victims of the formulas they receive, and if what they have accepted as truth is shown to be false or incomplete, they grow discouraged and lose faith; but the wise know that the verbal vesture of truth is a symbol which has but a proximate and relative value. The spirit is alive, and ceaselessly outgrows or transmutes the body with which it is clothed. What we can do with anything,—with money, knowledge, wealth,—depends on what we are. Ruskin prefers holy work to holy worship; but the antithesis is mistaken, for if worship is holy it impels to work, if work is holy it impels to worship. God's most sacred visible temple is a human body, and its profanation is the worst sacrilege.

All true belief, when we come to the last analysis, is belief in God, and the teacher of religion must keep this fact always in view.

The law of the struggle for life applies to opinions, beliefs, hopes, aims, ideals, just as it applies to individuals and species. Whatever survives, survives through conflict, because it is fit to survive. It does not follow, however, that the best survives, though we must think that in the end this is so, since we believe in God. When serious minds grapple with problems so remote from vulgar opinion that they seem to be meaningless or insoluble, the multitude, ever ready, like a crowd of boys, to mock and jeer, break forth into insult. These men, they cry are wicked, or they are fools.

In a society where it is assumed that all are equal, those who are really superior incur suspicion as though it were criminal to be different from the multitude; and hence they rarely win the favor of the crowd. The life-current of those who stir up a noise about them, runs shallow. The champion of the prize-ring or the race-course is hailed with shouts, for the crowd understand the achievement; but what can they know of the worth of a sage or a saint? The noblest struggles are of the mind and heart wrestling with unseen powers, with spirits, as St. Paul says, that they may compel them to give up the secret of truth and holiness. A glimpse of truth, a thrill of love, is better than the applause of a whole city. In striving steadfastly for thy own perfection and the happiness of others thou walkest and workest with God. Thy progress will help others to labor for their own, and the happiness thou givest will return to thee and become thine; and what is the will of God, if it is not the perfection and happiness of his children? To have merely enough strength to bear life's burden, to do the daily task, to face the cares which return with the sun and follow us into the night, is to be weak, is to lack the strong spirit for which work is light as play, and whose secret is heard in whispers by the hero and the saint. To be able to give joy and help to others we must have more life, wisdom, virtue, and happiness than we need for ourselves; and it is in giving joy and help to others that we ourselves receive increase of life, wisdom, virtue, and happiness. Be persuaded within thy deepest soul, that moral evil can never be good, and that sin can never be gain. So act that if all men acted as thou, all would be well. If to be like others is thy aim, thou art predestined to remain inferior. To be followed and applauded is to be diverted from one's work. Better alone with it in a garret than a guest in a banquet hall.

Let thy prayer be work and work thy prayer,
As God's truth and love are everywhere,
And whether by word or deed thou strive
In Him alone thou canst be alive.

If thou hast done thy best, God will give it worth.

If thou carest not for truth and love, for thee they are nothing worth; but it is because thou thyself art worthless. Wisdom and virtue is all thou lackest; of other things thou hast enough. When the passion for self-improvement is strong within us, all our relations to our fellow-men and nature receive new meaning and power, as opportunities to make ourselves what it is possible for us to become; and as we grow accustomed to take this view of whatever happens, we are made aware that disagreeable things are worth as much as the pleasant, that foes are as useful as friends. The obstacle arrests attention, provokes effort, and educates. It throws the light back upon the eye, and reveals the world of color and form; from it all sounds reverberate. We grow by overcoming; the force we conquer becomes our own. We rise on difficulties we surmount. What opposes, arouses, strengthens, and disciplines the will, discloses to the mind its power, and implants faith in the efficacy of patient, persevering labor. They who shrink from the combat are already defeated. To make everything easy is to smooth the way whereby we descend. To surround the young with what they ought themselves to achieve is to enfeeble and corrupt them. Happy is the poor man's son, who whithersoever he turns, sees the obstacle rise to challenge him to become a man; miserable the children of the rich, whose cursed-blessed fortune is an ever-present invitation to idleness and conceit. O mothers, you whose love is the best any of us have known, harden your sons, and urge them on, not in the race for wealth, but in the steep and narrow way wherein, through self-conquest and self-knowledge, they rise toward God and all high things. Nothing that has ever been said of your power tells the whole truth, and the only argument against you is the men who are your children. Education is always the result of personal influence. A mother, a father in the home, a pure and loving heart at the altar, a true man or woman in the school, a noble mind uttering itself in literature, which is personal thought and expression,—these are the forces which educate. Life proceeds from life, and religion, which is the highest power of life, can proceed only from God and religious souls. Not by preaching and teaching, but by living the life, can we make ourselves centres of spiritual influence.

Be like others, walk in the broad way, one of a herd, content to graze in a common pasture, believing equality man's highest law, though its meaning be equality with the brute. Is this our ideal? It is an atheistic creed. There is no God, there is nothing but matter, but atoms, and atoms are alike and equal,—let men be so too. To struggle with infinite faith and hope for some divine good is idolatry, is to believe in God; to be one's self is the unpardonable sin. It is thy aim to rise, to distinguish thyself; this means thou wouldst have higher place, more money, a greater house than thy neighbor's. It is a foolish ambition. Instead of trying to distinguish thyself, strive to become thyself, to make thyself worthy of the approval of God and wise men. "I am not to be pitied, my lord," said Bayard; "I die doing my duty." God has not given His world into thy keeping, but he has given thee to thyself to fashion and complete. If thou art busy seeking money or pleasure or praise, little time will remain wherein to seek and find thyself. They who are interesting to themselves, are interesting to themselves alone. The self-absorbed are the victims of mental and moral disease. The life which flows out to others, bearing light and warmth and fragrance, feels itself in the blessings it gives; that which is self-centred, stagnates like a pool, and becomes the habitation of doleful creatures.

There is a popularity which is born of the worship of noble deeds,—it is the best. There is another, which comes of the crowd's passion for what is noisy and spectacular,—it is the worst. The one is the popularity of heroes, the other that of charlatans.

Whatever thy chosen work, it is thy business to make thyself a man or a woman, and not a mere specialist; yet in following a specialty with enthusiasm, thou shalt go farther towards perfection and completeness of life than the multitude of pretenders, who are not in earnest about anything. Every harsh and unjust sentiment, every narrow and unworthy thought consented to and entertained, remains like a stain upon character. Whoever speaks or writes against freedom or knowledge or faith in God, or love of man or reverence of woman, but makes himself ridiculous; for men feel and believe that their true world is a world of high thoughts and noble sentiments, and they can neither respect nor trust those who strive to weaken their hold upon this world. Become thyself; do thy work. For this, all thy days are not too many or too long. If thou and it are worthy to be known, the presentation can be made in briefest time; and it matters little though it be deferred until after thy death.

Besides whatever other conditions, time is necessary to bring the best things to maturity, and to imagine that excellence demands less than life-long work, is to mistake. It is by the patient observation of the infinitesimal that science has done its best work; and it is only by unwearying attention to the thousand little things of life that we may hope to make some approach to moral and intellectual perfection. He who works with joy and cheerfulness in the field which himself has found and chosen, will acquire knowledge and skill, and his labor will be transformed into increase and newness of life.

We gain a clear view of things only when we set them apart from ourselves, and contemplate them simply as objects of thought. To see them aright we must be free from emotion and behold them in the cold air of the intellect. To look on them as in some way bound up with our personal good or evil, is to have the vision blurred. Study in the spirit of an investigator, who has no other than a scientific interest in what he sets himself to examine. The wise physician is wholly intent upon making a correct diagnosis, though the patient be his mother. What gain would self-delusion bring him or her he loves? Things are what they are, and it is our business to know them. Observe and hold thy judgment in suspense until patient looking shall have made truth so plain that to pass judgment is superfluous.

The aim of mental training is clearness and accuracy of view, together with the strength to keep steadfastly looking into the world of intelligible things. What rouses desire tends to enslave; what gives delight tends to liberate; the one appeals to the senses, the other to the soul. Hence, intellectual and moral pleasures alone are associated with the sense of freedom and pure joy. The lovers of freedom are as rare as the lovers of truth and of God. For most, liberty is but a trader's commodity, to be parted with for price, as their obedience is a slave's service. The chief good consists in acting justly and nobly, rather than in thinking acutely and profoundly. The free play of the mind is delightful, but the law of moral obligation is the deepest thing in us. Honor, place, and wealth, which are won at the price of self-improvement, the wise will not desire. Great opportunities seldom present themselves, but every moment of every hour of thy conscious life is an opportunity to improve thyself, which for thee is the best and most necessary thing. Since our power over others is small, but over ourselves large, let us devote our energies to self-improvement. "Nor let any man say," writes Locke, "he cannot govern his passions, nor hinder them from breaking out and carrying him into action; for what he can do before a prince or great man he can do alone or in the presence of God, if he will."

The sure way to happiness is to yield ourselves wholly to God, knowing that he has care of us, and at the same time to seek to draw from life whatever joy and delight it may bestow upon a high mind and a pure heart, receiving the blessing gladly, conscious all the while that what is external cannot really be ours, and is not, therefore, necessary to our contentment.

That many are wiser and stronger than thou, is not a motive for discouragement; the depressing thought is, that so few are wise and strong. He who gives his whole life to what he believes he is most capable of doing, succeeds, whatever be the worth of his work. There are many who are busy with many things; but one who has a high purpose, and who devotes all his energies to its fulfillment, is not easily found; and great and interesting characters are, therefore, rare.

To what better use can we put life than to employ it in ameliorating life? It is to this every wise and good man devotes himself, whether he be priest or teacher, physician or lawyer, philosopher or poet, captain of industry or statesman.

Chapter V.

The Scope of Public-School Education.

Our system of Public-School Education is a result of the faith of the people in the need of universal intelligence for the maintenance of popular government. Does this system include moral training? Since the teaching of religious doctrines is precluded, this, I imagine, is what we are to consider in discussing the Scope of Public-School Education. The equivalents of scope are aim, end, opportunity, range of view; and the equivalents of education are training, discipline, development, instruction. The proper meaning of the word education, it seems, is not a drawing out, but a training up, as vines are trained to lay hold of and rise by means of what is stronger than themselves. My subject, then, is the aim, end, opportunity, and range of view of public-school education, which to be education at all, in any true sense, must be a training, discipline, development, and instruction of man's whole being, physical, intellectual, and moral. This, I suppose, is what Herbert Spencer means when he defines education to be a preparation for complete living. Montaigne says the end of education is wisdom and virtue; Comenius declares it to be knowledge, virtue, and religion; Milton, likeness to God through virtue and faith; Locke, health of body, virtue, and good manners; Herbart, virtue, which is the realization in each one of the idea of inner freedom; while Kant and Fichte declare it to consist chiefly in the formation of character. All these thinkers agree that the supreme end of education is spiritual or ethical. The controlling aim, then, should be, not to impart information, but to upbuild the being which makes us human, to form habits of right thinking and doing. The ideal is virtually that of Israel,—that righteousness is life,—though the Greek ideal of beauty and freedom may not be excluded. It is the doctrine that manners make the man, that conduct is three-fourths of life, leaving but one-fourth for intellectual activity and æsthetic enjoyment; and into this fourth of life but few ever enter in any real way, while all are called and may learn to do good and avoid evil.

"In the end," says Ruskin, "the God of heaven and earth loves active, modest, and kind people, and hates idle, proud, greedy, and cruel ones." We can all learn to become active, modest, and kind; to turn from idleness, pride, greed, and cruelty. But we cannot all make ourselves capable of living in the high regions of pure thought and ideal beauty; and for the few even who are able to do this, it is still true that conduct is three-fourths of life.

"The end of man," says Büchner, "is conversion into carbonic acid, water, and ammonia." This also is an ideal, and he thinks we should be pleased to know that in dying we give back to the universe what had been lent. He moralizes too; but if all we can know of our destiny is that we shall be converted into carbonic acid, water, and ammonia, the sermon may be omitted. On such a faith it is not possible to found a satisfactory system of education. Men will always refuse to think thus meanly of themselves, and in answer to those who would persuade them that they are but brutes, they will, with perfect confidence, claim kinship with God; for from an utterly frivolous view of life both our reason and our instinct turn.

The Scope of Public-School Education is to co-operate with the physical, social, and religious environment to form good and wise men and women. Unless we bear in mind that the school is but one of several educational agencies, we shall not form a right estimate of its office. It depends almost wholly for its success upon the kind of material furnished it by the home, the state, and the church; and, to confine our view to our own country, I have little hesitation in affirming that our home life, our social and political life, and our religious life have contributed far more to make us what we are than any and all of our schools. The school, unless it works in harmony with these great forces, can do little more than sharpen the wits. Many of the teachers of our Indian schools are doubtless competent and earnest; but their pupils, when they return to their tribes, quickly lose what they have gained, because they are thrown into an environment which annuls the ideals that prevailed in the school. The controlling aim of our teachers should be, therefore, to bring their pedagogical action into harmony with what is best in the domestic, social, and religious life of the child; for this is the foundation on which they must build, and to weaken it is to expose the whole structure to ruin. Hence the teacher's attitude toward the child should be that of sympathy with him in his love for his parents, his country, and his religion. His reason is still feeble, and his life is largely one of feeling; and the fountain-heads of his purest and noblest feelings are precisely his parents, his country, and his religion, and to tamper with them is to poison the wells whence he draws the water of life. To assume and hold this attitude with sincerity and tact is difficult; it requires both character and culture; it implies a genuine love of mankind and of human excellence; reverence for whatever uplifts, purifies, and strengthens the heart; knowledge of the world, of literature, and of history, united with an earnest desire to do whatever may be possible to lead each pupil toward life in its completeness, which is health and healthful activity of body and mind and heart and soul.

As the heart makes the home, the teacher makes the school. What we need above all things, wherever the young are gathered for education, is not a showy building, or costly apparatus, or improved methods or text-books, but a living, loving, illumined human being who has deep faith in the power of education and a real desire to bring it to bear upon those who are intrusted to him. This applies to the primary school with as much force as to the high school and university. Those who think, and they are, I imagine, the vast majority, that any one who can read and write, who knows something of arithmetic, geography, and history, is competent to educate young children, have not even the most elementary notions of what education is.

What the teacher is, not what he utters and inculcates, is the important thing. The life he lives, and whatever reveals that life to his pupils; his unconscious behavior, even; above all, what in his inmost soul he hopes, believes, and loves, have far deeper and more potent influence than mere lessons can ever have. It is precisely here that we Americans, whose talent is predominantly practical and inventive, are apt to go astray. We have won such marvellous victories with our practical sense and inventive genius that we have grown accustomed to look to them for aid, whatever the nature of the difficulty or problem may be. Machinery can be made to do much, and to do well what it does. With its help we move rapidly; we bring the ends of the earth into instantaneous communication; we print the daily history of the world and throw it before every door; we plough and we sow and we reap; we build cities, and we fill our houses with whatever conduces to comfort or luxury. All this and much more machinery enables us to do. But it cannot create life, nor can it, in any effective way, promote vital processes. Now, education is essentially a vital process. It is a furthering of life; and as the living proceed from the living, they can rise into the wider world of ideas and conduct only by the help of the living; and as in the physical realm every animal begets after its own likeness, so also in the spiritual the teacher can give but what he has. If the well-spring of truth and love has run dry within himself, he teaches in vain. His words will no more bring forth life than desert winds will clothe arid sands with verdure. Much talking and writing about education have chiefly helped to obscure a matter which is really plain. The purpose of the public school is or should be not to form a mechanic or a specialist of any kind, but to form a true man or woman. Hence the number of things we teach the child is of small moment. Those schools, in fact, in which the greatest number of things are taught give, as a rule, the least education. The character of the Roman people, which enabled them to dominate the earth and to give laws to the world, was formed before they had schools, and when their schools were most flourishing they themselves were in rapid moral and social dissolution. We make education and religion too much a social affair, and too little a personal affair. Their essence lies in their power to transform the individual, and it is only in transforming him that they recreate the wider life of the community. The Founder of Christianity addressed himself to the individual, and gave little heed to the state or other environment. He looked to a purified inner source of life to create for itself a worthier environment, and simply ignored devices for working sudden and startling changes. They who have entered into the hidden meaning of this secret and this method turn in utter incredulity from the schemes of declaimers and agitators.

The men who fill the world, each with his plan for reforming and saving it, may have their uses, since the poet tells us there are uses in adversity, which, like the toad, ugly and venomous, wears yet a precious jewel in its head; but to one deafened by their discordant and clamorous voices, the good purpose they serve seems to be as mythical as the jewel in the toad's head.

Have not those who mistake their crotchets for Nature's laws invaded our schools? Have they not succeeded in forming a public opinion and in setting devices at work which render education, in the true sense of the word, if not impossible, difficult? Literature is a criticism of life, made by those who are in love with life, and have the deepest faith in its possibilities; and all criticism which is inspired by sympathy and faith and controlled by knowledge is helpful. Complacent thoughts are rarely true, and hardly ever useful. It is a prompting of nature to turn from what we have to what we lack, for thus only is there hope of amendment and progress. We are, to quote Emerson,

> "Built of furtherance and pursuing,
> Not of spent deeds, but of doing."

Hence the wise and the strong dwell not upon their virtues and accomplishments, but strive to learn wherein they fail, for it is in correcting this they desire to labor. They wish to know the truth about themselves, are willing to try to see themselves as others see them, that self-knowledge may make self-improvement possible. They turn from flattery, for they understand that flattery is insult. Now, if this is the attitude of wise and strong men, how much more should it not be that of a wise and strong people? Whenever persons or things are viewed as related in some special way to ourselves, our opinions of them will hardly be free from bias. When, for instance, I think or speak of my country, my religion, my friends, my enemies, I find it difficult to put away the prejudice which my self-esteem and vanity create, and which, like a haze, ever surrounds me to color or obscure the pure light of reason. It cannot do us harm to have our defects and shortcomings pointed out to us; but to be told by demagogues and declaimers that we are the greatest, the most enlightened, the most virtuous people which exists or has existed, can surely do us no good. If it is true, we should not dwell upon it, for this will but distract us from striving for the things in which we are deficient; and if it is false, it can only mislead us and nourish a foolish conceit. It is the orator's misfortune to be compelled to think of his audience rather than of truth. It is his business to please, persuade, and convince; and men are pleased with flattering lies, persuaded and convinced by appeals to passion and interest. Happier is the writer, who need not think of a reader, but finds his reward in the truth he expresses.

It is not possible for an enlightened mind not to take profound interest in our great system of public education. To do this he need not think it the best system. He may deem it defective in important requisites. He may hold, as I hold, that the system is of minor importance, the kind of teacher being all important. But if he loves his country, if he loves human excellence, if he has faith in man's capacity for growth, he cannot but turn his thoughts, with abiding attention and sympathy, to the generous and determined efforts of a powerful and vigorous people to educate themselves. Were our public-school system nothing more than the nation's profession of faith in the transforming power of education, it would be an omen of good and a ground for hope; and one cannot do more useful work than to help to form a public opinion which will accept with thankfulness the free play of all sincere minds about this great question, and which will cause the genuine lovers of our country to turn in contempt from the clamors politicians and bigots are apt to raise when an honest man utters honest thought on this all-important subject.

I am willing to assume and to accept as a fact that our theological differences make it impossible to introduce the teaching of any religious creed into the public school. I take the system as it is,—that is, as a system of secular education,—and I address myself more directly to the question proposed: What is or should be its scope?

The fact that religious instruction is excluded makes it all the more necessary that humanizing and ethical aims should be kept constantly in view. Whoever teaches in a public school should be profoundly convinced that man is more than an animal which may be taught cunning and quickness. A weed in blossom may have a certain beauty, but it will bear no fruit; and so the boy or youth one often meets, with his irreverent smartness, his precocious pseudo-knowledge of a hundred things, may excite a kind of interest, but he gives little promise of a noble future. The flower of his life is the blossom of the weed, which in its decay will poison the air, or, at the best, serve but to fertilize the soil. If we are to work to good purpose we must take our stand, with the great thinkers and educators, on the broad field of man's nature, and act in the light of the only true ideal of education,—that its end is wisdom, virtue, knowledge, power, reverence, faith, health, behavior, hope, and love; in a word, whatever powers and capacities make for intelligence, for conduct, for character, for completeness of life. Not for a moment should we permit ourselves to be deluded by the thought that because the teaching of religious creeds is excluded, therefore we may make no appeal to the fountain-heads which sleep within every breast, the welling of whose waters alone has power to make us human. If we are forbidden to turn the current into this or that channel, we are not forbidden to recognize the universal truth that man lives by faith, hope, and love, by imagination and desire, and that it is precisely for this reason that he is educable. We move irresistibly in the lines of our real faith and desire, and the educator's great purpose is to help us to believe in what is high and to desire what is good. Since for the irreverent and vulgar spirit nothing is high or good, reverence, and the refinement which is the fruit of true intelligence, urge ceaselessly their claims on the teacher's attention. Goethe, I suppose, was little enough of a Christian to satisfy the demands of an agnostic cripple even, and yet he held that the best thing in man is the thrill of awe; and that the chief business of education is to cultivate reverence for whatever is above, beneath, around, and within us. This he believed to be the only philosophical and healthful attitude of mind and heart towards the universe, seen and unseen. May not the meanest flower that blows bring thoughts that lie too deep for tears? Is not reverence a part of all the sweetest and purest feelings which bind us to father and mother, to friends and home and country? Is it not the very bloom and fragrance, not only of the highest religious faith, but also of the best culture? Let the thrill of awe cease to vibrate, and you will have a world in which money is more than man, office better than honesty, and books like "Innocents Abroad" or "Peck's Bad Boy" more indicative of the kind of man we form than are the noblest works of genius. What is the great aim of the primary school, if it is not the nutrition of feeling? The child is weak in mind, weak in will, but he is most impressionable. Feeble in thought, he is strong in capacity to feel the emotions which are the sap of the tree of moral life. He responds quickly to the appeals of love, tenderness, and sympathy. He is alive to whatever is noble, heroic, and venerable. He desires the approbation of others, especially of those whom he believes to be true and high and pure, he has unquestioning faith, not only in God but in great men, who, for him, indeed, are earthly gods. Is not his father a divine man, whose mere word drives away all fear and fills him with confidence? The touch of his mother's hand stills his pain; if he is frightened, her voice is enough to soothe him to sleep. To imagine that we are educating this being of infinite sensibility and impressionability when we do little else than teach him to read, write, and cipher, is to cherish a delusion. It is not his destiny to become a reading, writing, and ciphering machine, but to become a man who believes, hopes, and loves; who holds to sovereign truth, and is swayed by sympathy; who looks up with reverence and awe to the heavens, and hearkens with cheerful obedience to the call of duty; who has habits of right thinking and well doing which have become a law unto him, a second nature. And if it be said that we all recognize this to be so, but that it is not the business of the school to help to form such a man; that it does its work when it sharpens the wits, I will answer with the words of William von Humboldt: "Whatever we wish to see introduced into the life of a nation must first be introduced into its schools."

Now, what we wish to see introduced into the life of the nation is not the power of shrewd men, wholly absorbed in the striving for wealth, reckless of the means by which it is gotten, and who, whether they succeed or whether they fail, look upon money as the equivalent of the best things man knows or has; who therefore think that the highest purpose of government, as of other social forces and institutions, is to make it easy for all to get abundance of gold and to live in sloven plenty; but what we wish to see introduced into the life of the nation is the power of intelligence and virtue, of wisdom and conduct. We believe, and in fact know, that humanity, justice, truthfulness, honesty, honor, fidelity, courage, integrity, reverence, purity, and self-respect are higher and mightier than anything mere sharpened wits can accomplish. But if these virtues, which constitute nearly the whole sum of man's strength and worth, are to be introduced into the life of the nation, they must be introduced into the schools, into the process of education. We must recognize, not in theory alone but in practice, that the chief end of education is ethical, since conduct is three-fourths of human life. The aim must be to make men true in thought and word, pure in desire, faithful in act, upright in deed; men who understand that the highest good does not lie in the possession of anything whatsoever, but that it lies in power and quality of being; for whom what we are and not what we have is the guiding principle; who know that the best work is not that for which we receive most pay, but that which is most favorable to life, physical, moral, intellectual, and religious; since man does not exist for work or the Sabbath, but work and rest exist for him, that he may thrive and become more human and more divine. We must cease to tell boys and girls that education will enable them to get hold of the good things of which they believe the world to be full; we must make them realize rather that the best thing in the world is a noble man or woman, and to be that is the only certain way to a worthy and contented life. All talk about patriotism which implies that it is possible to be a patriot or a good citizen without being a true and good man, is sophistical and hollow. How shall he who cares not for his better self care for his country?

We must look, as educators, most closely to those sides of the national life where there is the greatest menace of ruin. It is plain that our besetting sin, as a people, is not intemperance or unchastity, but dishonesty. From the watering and manipulating of stocks to the adulteration of food and drink, from the booming of towns and lands to the selling of votes and the buying of office, from the halls of Congress to the policeman's beat, from the capitalist who controls trusts and syndicates to the mechanic who does inferior work, the taint of dishonesty is everywhere. We distrust one another, distrust those who manage public affairs, distrust our own fixed will to suffer the worst that may befall rather than cheat or steal or lie. Dishonesty hangs, like mephitic air, about our newspapers, our legislative assemblies, the municipal government of our towns and cities, about our churches even, since our religion itself seems to lack that highest kind of honesty, the downright and thorough sincerity which is its life-breath.

If the teacher in the public school may not insist that an honest man is the noblest work of God, he may teach at least that he who fails in honesty fails in the most essential quality of manhood, enters into warfare with the forces which have made him what he is, and which secure him the possession of what he holds dearer than himself, since he barters for it his self-respect; that the dishonest man is an anarchist and dissocialist, one who does what in him lies to destroy credit, and the sense of the sacredness of property, obedience to law, and belief in the rights of man. If our teachers are to work in the light of an ideal, if they are to have a conscious end in view, as all who strive intelligently must have, if they are to hold a principle which will give unity to their methods, they must seek it in the idea of morality, of conduct, which is three-fourths of life.

I myself am persuaded that the real and philosophical basis of morality is the being of God, a being absolute, infinite, unimaginable, inconceivable, of whom our highest and nearest thought is that he is not only almighty, but all-wise and all-good as well. But it is possible, I think, to cultivate the moral sense without directly and expressly assigning to it this philosophical and religious basis; for goodness is largely its own evidence, as virtue is its own reward. It all depends on the teacher. Life produces life, life develops life; and if the teacher have within himself a living sense of the all-importance of conduct, if he thoroughly realize that what we call knowledge is but a small part of man's life, his influence will nourish the feelings by which character is evolved. The germ of a moral idea is always an emotion, and that which impels to right action is the emotion rather than the idea. The teachings of the heart remain forever, and they are the most important; for what we love, genuinely believe in, and desire decides what we are and may become. Hence the true educator, even in giving technical instruction, strives not merely to make a workman, but to make also a man, whose being shall be touched to finer issues by spiritual powers, who shall be upheld by faith in the worth and sacredness of life, and in the education by which it is transformed, enriched, purified, and ennobled. He understands that an educated man, who, in the common acceptation of the phrase, is one who knows something, who knows many things, is, in truth, simply one who has acquired habits of right thinking and right doing. The culture which we wish to see prevail throughout our country is not learning and literary skill; it is character and intellectual openness,—that higher humanity which is latent within us all; which is power, wisdom, truth, goodness, love, sympathy, grace, and beauty; whose surpassing excellence the poor may know as well as the rich; whose charm the multitude may feel as well as the chosen few.

"He who speaks of the people," says Guicciardini, "speaks, in sooth, of a foolish animal, a prey to a thousand errors, a thousand confusions, without taste, without affection, without firmness." The scope of our public-school education is to make common-places of this kind, by which all literature is pervaded, so false as to be absurd; and when this end shall have been attained, Democracy will have won its noblest victory.

How shall we find the secret from which hope of such success will spring? By so forming and directing the power of public opinion, of national approval, and of money, as to make the best men and women willing and ready to enter the teacher's profession. The kind of man who educates is the test of the kind of education given, and there is properly no other test. When we Americans shall have learned to believe with all our hearts and with all the strength of irresistible conviction that a true educator is a more important, in every way a more useful, sort of man than a great railway king, or pork butcher, or captain of industry, or grain buyer, or stock manipulator, we shall have begun to make ourselves capable of perceiving the real scope of public-school education.

Chapter VI.

The Religious Element in Education.

The theory of development, which is now widely received and applied to all things, from star dust to the latest fashion, is at once a sign and a cause of the almost unlimited confidence which we put in the remedial and transforming power of education. We no longer think of God as standing aloof from nature and the course of history. He it is who works in the play of atoms and in the throbbings of the human heart; and as we perceive his action in the evolution both of matter and of mind, we know and feel that, when with conscious purpose we strive to call forth and make living the latent powers of man's being, we are working with him in the direction in which he impels the universe. Education, therefore, we look upon as necessary, not merely because it is indispensable to any high and human kind of life, but also because God has made development the law both of conscious and unconscious nature. He is in act all that the finite may become, and the effort to grow in strength, knowledge, and virtue springs from a divine impulse.

Although we know that the earth is not the centre of the universe, that it is but a minor satellite, a globule lost in space, our deepest thought still finds that the end of nature is the production of rational beings, of man; for the final reason for which all things exist is that the infinite good may be communicated; and since the highest good is truth and holiness, it can be communicated only to beings who think and love. Hence all things are man's, and he exists that he may make himself like God; in other words, that he may educate himself; for the end of education is to fit him for completeness of life, to train all his faculties, to call all his endowments into play, to make him symmetrical and whole in body and soul. This, of course, is the ideal, and consequently the unattainable; but in the light of ideals alone do we see rightly and judge truly; and to take a lower view of the aim and end of education is to take a partial view. To hold that God is, and that man truly lives only in so far as he is made partaker of the divine life, is, by implication, to hold that his education should be primarily and essentially religious. Our opinions and beliefs, however, are never the result of purely rational processes, and hence a mere syllogism has small persuasive force, or even no influence at all, upon our way of looking at things, or the motives which determine action.

As it is useless to argue against the nature of things, so we generally plead in vain when our world-view is other than that of those whom we seek to convince; for those who observe from different points either do not see the same objects or do not see them in the same light. Life is complex, and the springs of thought and action are controlled in mysterious ways by forces and impulses which we neither clearly understand nor accurately measure. What is called the spirit of the age, the spirit which, as the Poet says, sits at the roaring loom of time and weaves for God the garment whereby He is made visible to us, exercises a potent influence upon all our thinking and doing. We live in an era of progress, and progress means differentiation of structure and specialization of function. The more perfect the organism, the more are its separate functions assigned to separate parts. As social aggregates develop, a similar differentiation takes place. Offices which were in the hands of one are distributed among several. Agencies are evolved by which processes of production, distribution, and exchange are carried on. Trades and professions are called into existence. As enlightenment and skill increase, men become more difficult to please. They demand the best work, and the best work can be done, as a rule, only by specialists. Specialization thus becomes a characteristic of civilization. The patriarch is both king and priest. In Greece and Rome, religion is a function of the State. In the Middle Age, the Church and the State coalesce, and form such an intimate union that the special domain of either is invaded by both. But differentiation finally takes place, and we all learn to distinguish between the things of Cæsar and the things of God. This separation has far-reaching results. In asserting its independence, the State was driven to use argument as well as force. Thus learning, which in the confusion that succeeded the incursions of the Barbarians was cultivated almost exclusively by ecclesiastics, grew to be of interest and importance to laymen. They began to study, and the subjects which most engaged their thoughts were not religious, in the accepted sense of the word. The Protestant rebellion is but a phase of this revolution. It began with the introduction of the literature of Greece into Western Europe.

The spirit of inquiry and mental curiosity was thereby awakened in wider circles; enthusiasm for the truth and beauty to which Greek genius has given the most perfect expression, was aroused; and interest in intellectual and artistic culture was called forth. New ideals were upheld to fresh and wondering minds. The contagion spread, and the thirst for knowledge was carried to ever-widening spheres. It thus came to pass that the cleric and the scholar ceased to be identical. The boundaries of knowledge were enlarged when the inductive method was applied to the study of nature, and it soon became impossible for one man to pretend to a mastery of all science. And so the principle of the division of labor was introduced into things of the intellect. Of old, the prophet or the philosopher was supposed to possess all wisdom; but now it had become plain that proficiency could be hoped for only by lifelong devotion to some special branch of knowledge. This led to other developments. The business of teaching, which had been almost exclusively in the hands of ecclesiastics, was now necessarily taken up by laymen also. As feudalism fell to decay, and the assertion of popular rights began to point to the advent of democracy, the movement in opposition to privilege logically led to the claim that learning should no longer be held to be the appanage of special classes, but that the gates of the temple of knowledge should be thrown open to the whole people. To make education universal, the most ready and the simplest means was to levy a school tax; and as this could be done only by the State, the State established systems of education and assumed the office of teacher. The result of all this has been that the school, which throughout Christendom is the creation of the church, has in most countries very largely passed into the control of the civil government.

This transference of control need not, however, involve the exclusion of religious influence and instruction; though once the State has gained the ascendency, the natural tendency is to take a partial and secular view of the whole question of education, and to limit the functions of the school to the training of the mental faculties. And, as a matter of fact, this tendency is found in men of widely differing and even conflicting opinions and convictions concerning religion itself. It is most pronounced, however, in the educational theories and systems of positivists and agnostics. As they hold that there is no God, or that we cannot know that there is a God, they necessarily conclude that it is absurd to attempt to teach children anything about God. This view is forcibly expressed by Issaurat, a French writer on education, in a recently published volume, which he calls "The Evolution and History of Pedagogy."

"All religion," he affirms, in the concluding chapter of his book, "impedes, thwarts, misdirects, and troubles the natural education of man, the normal and harmonious development of his physical, moral, and intellectual faculties; and since educational reform is not possible without reformation in the government, it is the duty of the State, not merely to separate itself from the church, but to suppress the church and to found the science of education upon biological philosophy, upon transformism—let us say the word, upon materialism." This view is manifestly the inevitable result of Issaurat's general system of thought and belief. In his opinion, matter alone really exists, and what is called spirit is but a phase of its evolution. The world of spirit, therefore, is illusory; and to bring up the young to believe that it is the infinite, essential reality, is to teach them what is false, and to give a wrong direction to the whole course of life. For practical purposes this is the view not only of materialists and positivists, but of agnostics as well, who, though they do not deny the existence of spirit, assert that only the phenomenal can be known, or become the subject-matter of teaching. They all agree in holding that the theological world-view was the primitive one, which, yielding to the metaphysical, has been finally superseded by the scientific, the sole basis of a rational philosophy. The ideas of God, substance, cause, and end, are metaphysical ideas, which, if we wish to understand nature, must be ignored; for the study of nature is the study simply of facts and their relations with one another. There is, so they think, no such thing as substance, any more than there is such a thing as a principle of gravity, heat, light, electricity, or chemical affinity. The vital principle too, which has played so great a part in physiological inquiries, must be given up; and therefore, while nearly all the philosophers, from Kant to our own day, have made psychology the foundation of the science of education, there is at present a marked tendency to have it rest solely on biology. Whether and to what extent these theories are true or false, is beyond the purpose of this argument. True or false, they fairly describe the views of a large number of thinkers in our day, and enable us to form a conception of their philosophy of education. "Why trouble ourselves," asks Professor Huxley, "about matters of which, however important they may be, we do know nothing and can know nothing? With a view to our duty in this life, it is necessary to be possessed of only two beliefs: The first, that the order of nature is ascertainable by our faculties to an extent that is practically unlimited; the second, that our volition counts for something as a condition of the course of events." Our volition counts as a condition, but it is after all only a part of the course of events, and, consequently, the only belief it is necessary to hold is, that the course of events is ascertainable by our faculties to a practically unlimited extent. Such is the brief creed of materialists and agnostics. The order of nature is the only known god, and man's sole end and duty is to make himself acquainted with it, that through obedience he may attain the highest perfection and happiness of which he is capable. This is the one true religion, and an enlightened people should forbid that any other be taught in their schools. Here we have an intelligible and well-defined position, and the one which, from the point of view of such men as Issaurat and Huxley, is alone tenable.

Every one now, who thinks at all, has some theory of the world, and hence the shades of unbelief as of belief are many; and since views of education are part of a more general system of philosophy, it is inevitable that those who disagree upon the fundamental questions of thought, disagree also in their notions as to what is the school's proper office.

Materialists, pantheists, positivists, secularists, and pessimists unite in denying that there is a God above and distinct from nature, while agnostics and cosmists affirm that such a being, if he exist, must necessarily lie outside the domain of knowledge. Positive religious doctrines, therefore, are superstition. As these views are reflected in a more or less vague way in the writings of the multitude of those who make the current literature, public opinion becomes averse to religious dogmas. A large number of cultivated minds turn from all definite systems, whether of thought or belief. Everything may be tolerated, if only the spirit of dogmatism is away. They recognize how great a thing religion is, how profoundly it touches life, how powerfully it shapes conduct. Without it, civilization is hard and mechanical, art is formal and feeble, and man himself but a shrewd animal. But, from their points of view, doctrines about God and Christ and the church have nothing to do with religion. To think of God as substance is to convert him into nature, to think of him as a person is to limit him. The only absolute is the moral order of the world. The religion of Christ is not a theory or a system of thought; it is a view of life, and its essence is found in belief in the reality of moral ideas. The supernatural may fall away,—even the notion of a Providence which rules the world in the interest of the good may be given up,—and we still have the method and the secret of Jesus, all that is of value in his life and teaching. All theology is an illusion, all creeds are a mistake. Religion rests upon the moral power, which is not a conclusion drawn from facts, but the fact itself,—the primal and essential fact in human life. Religion is simply morality suffused by the glow and warmth of a devout and reverent temper, and to teach doctrines about God and the church will not make men religious.

It is obvious to object that morality supposes belief in a Personal God and in the soul of man, as law implies a law-giver. This objection is meaningless, not only for the thinkers whom I have mentioned, but for others who find little interest in the literary and religious ideas of such men as Matthew Arnold. Morality, they claim, is independent, not only of metaphysics, but of religion as well. It is a science, as yet, indeed, imperfectly developed, but a science nevertheless, just as chemistry or physiology is a science. Human acts are controlled, not by a higher will or man's freedom of choice, but by physical laws. The peculiarity of this view does not lie in the contention that ethics is a science, but in the claim that it is a science altogether independent of metaphysical and religious dogmas. All forces, it is asserted, physical, mental, and moral, are identical; and morality, like bodily vigor, is a product of organism. It is, in fact, but an elaboration of the two radical instincts of nutrition and propagation, from which springs the twofold movement of conscious life, the egoistic and the altruistic. This theory is accepted alike in the German school of materialism, in the French school of positivism, and in the English school of utilitarianism. What the influence of modern empiricism upon American opinion may be, it is difficult to determine. Americans certainly are a practical people, but they are not devoid of interest in speculative views. More than any other people, possibly, they have faith in the marvellous things which science is destined to accomplish, and they willingly listen to men of science, even when they quit the regions of fact for those of opinion. Thus the various theories, to which the progress of natural knowledge has given rise, are received by them, if not with implicit trust, with a kind of feeling, at least, that they may be true.

There is even a disposition to treat doubts of the truth of Christianity as a mark of intellectual vigor, and sometimes as a sign of religious sincerity. Preoccupied with material interests, but yet finding time to read the thoughts of many minds and to hear the discussion of antagonistic opinions and systems, they find it difficult to trust with entire confidence to what they know or believe. It all seems to be relative, and another generation may see everything in a different light. Problems take the place of principles, religious convictions are feeble, the grasp of Christian truth is relaxed, and the result is a certain moral hesitancy and infirmity.

They are not hostile to the churches, but they are more or less indifferent to their doctrines. As each sect has its peculiar creed, the dogmatic position of the church is thought to be of little moment. The important thing is to promote intelligence and virtue. The distinctively sectarian view they look upon as narrow and false, and the good which ecclesiastical organizations do is done in spite of their characteristic doctrines. The note of sectarianism is to them what the note of provincialism is to a man of culture, or lack of breeding to a gentleman. The moral fervor, which sectarians more than others feel, is, they freely grant, a power for good. It has a wholesome influence upon character, and is a support of the virtues which make free institutions possible, and which alone can make them permanent. But it has no necessary connection with theological doctrines, since it is found in earnest believers, whatever their creed. It is the child of enthusiastic faith, and is nourished and kept living by worship, not by dogmatic asseverations. As the power of the churches does not lie in their creeds, to make these creeds a school lesson cannot be desirable, especially when we reflect that the method of religion and the method of science are at variance.

Such, I imagine, are the views of large numbers of Americans, who are not members of any church, but whose influence is strongly felt in political and commercial as well as in social and professional life. And numbers of zealous Protestants are in substantial agreement with them, since they hold that faith is an emotional rather than an intellectual state of mind, and that religion is not so much a way of thinking as a way of feeling and acting. They assume, of course, as the prerequisites of religious belief, the dogmas of the existence of a personal God and of an immortal human soul; but, for the rest, they lay stress upon conduct and piety, not upon orthodox faith. A church must have a creed, as a party must have a platform; but unhesitating confidence in the truth of the doctrines which it thus formulates is not indispensable. American churches tend to ignore creeds. This is due, in a measure, to the growing desire to form a union among the several sects; but it is none the less a sign of waning belief in dogmatic religion. Hence the increasing emphasis which preaching lays upon the moral, æsthetic, and emotional aspects of the religious life. Hence, too, the assumption that the soul of the church may live, though the body be dead.

But, apart from all theories and systems of belief and thought, public opinion in America sets strongly against the denominational school.

The question of education is considered from a practical rather than from a theoretical point of view, and public sentiment on the subject may be embodied in the following words: The civilized world now recognizes the necessity of popular education. In a government of the people, such as this is, intelligence should be universal. In such a government, to be ignorant is not merely to be weak, it is also to be dangerous to the common welfare; for the ignorant are not only the victims of circumstances, they are the instruments which unscrupulous and designing men make use of, to taint the source of political authority and to thwart the will of the people. To protect itself, the State is forced to establish schools and to see that all acquire at least the rudiments of letters. This is so plain a case that argument becomes ridiculous. They who doubt the good of knowledge are not to be reasoned with, and in America not to see that it is necessary, is to know nothing of our political, commercial, and social life. But the American State can give only a secular education, for it is separate from the church, and its citizens profess such various and even conflicting beliefs, that in establishing a school system, it is compelled to eliminate the question of religion. Church and State are separate institutions, and their functions are different and distinct. The church seeks to turn men from sin, that they may become pleasing to God and save their souls; the State takes no cognizance of sin, but strives to prevent crime, and to secure to all its citizens the enjoyment of life, liberty, and property. Americans are a Christian people. Religious zeal impelled their ancestors to the New World, and when schools were first established here, they were established by the churches, and religious instruction formed an important part of the education they gave. This was natural, and it was desirable even, in primitive times, when each colony had its own creed and worship, when society was simple, and the State as yet imperfectly organized. Here, as in the Old World, the school was the daughter of the church, and she has doubtless rendered invaluable service to civilization, by fostering a love for knowledge among barbarous races and in struggling communities. But the task of maintaining a school system such as the requirements of a great and progressive nation demands, is beyond her strength. This is so, at least, when the church is split into jealous and warring sects.

To introduce the spirit of sectarianism into the class-room would destroy the harmony and good-will among citizens, which it is one of the aims of the common school to cherish. There is, besides, no reason why this should be done, since the family and the church give all the religious instruction which children are capable of receiving.

This, it seems to me, is a fair presentation of the views and ideas which go to the making of current American opinion on the question of religious instruction in State schools; and current opinion, when the subject-matter is not susceptible of physical demonstration, cannot be turned suddenly in an opposite direction. When men have grown accustomed to look at things in a certain way, they have acquired a mental habit, which no mere argument, however cogent or eloquent, is able to overcome. To what extent this view of the school question prevails is readily perceived by whoever recalls to mind that not one of the States of the Union has attempted to introduce the denominational system of education, while all the political parties have bound themselves to uphold the present purely secular system. The opinion that the prosperity of the nation depends upon the intelligence and activity of the people, and to no appreciable extent upon the influence of ecclesiastical organizations, has so far prevailed, that the general feeling has come to be that the State has no direct interest in the church, which is the concern merely of individuals. The religious denominations themselves have helped to inspire this sentiment by their jealousies and rivalries. The smaller sects feel that State aid for denominational schools would accrue to the benefit chiefly of the larger; and the others are willing to forego favors which they could not receive without permitting the Catholic Church to participate also in the bounty of the government.

The Catholic view of the school question is as clearly defined as it is well known. It rests upon the general ground that man is created for a supernatural end, and that the church is the divinely appointed agency to help him to attain his supreme destiny. If education is a training for completeness of life, its primary element is the religious, for complete life is life in God. Hence we may not assume an attitude toward the child, whether in the home, in the church, or in the school, which might imply that life apart from God could be anything else than broken and fragmentary. A complete man is not one whose mind only is active and enlightened; but he is a complete man who is alive in all his faculties. The truly human is found not in knowledge alone, but also in faith, in hope, in love, in pure-mindedness, in reverence, in the sense of beauty, in devoutness, in the thrill of awe, which Goethe says is the highest thing in man. If the teacher is forbidden to touch upon religion, the source of these noble virtues and ideal moods is sealed. His work and influence become mechanical, and he will form but commonplace and vulgar men. And if an educational system is established on this narrow and material basis, the result will be deterioration of the national type, and the loss of the finer qualities which make men many-sided and interesting, which are the safeguards of personal purity and of unselfish conduct.

Religion is the vital element in character, and to treat it as though it were but an incidental phase of man's life is to blunder in a matter of the highest and most serious import. Man is born to act, and thought is valuable mainly as a guide to action. Now, the chief inspiration to action, and above all to right action, is found in faith, hope, and love, the virtues of religion, and not in knowledge, the virtue of the intellect. Knowledge, indeed, is effectual only when it is loved, believed in, and held to be a ground for hope. Man does not live on bread alone, and if he is brought up to look to material things, as to the chief good, his higher faculties will be stunted. If to do rightly rather than to think keenly is man's chief business here on earth, then the virtues of religion are more important than those of the intellect; for to think is to be unresolved, whereas to believe is to be impelled in the direction of one's faith. In epochs of doubt things fall to decay; in epochs of faith the powers which make for full and vigorous life, hold sway. The education which forms character is indispensable, that which trains the mind is desirable. The essential element in human life is conduct, and conduct springs from what we believe, cling to, love, and yearn for, vastly more than from what we know. The decadence and ruin of individuals and of societies come from lack of virtue, not from lack of knowledge. "The hard and valuable part of education," says Locke, "is virtue; this is the solid and substantial good, which the teacher should never cease to inculcate till the young man places his strength, his glory, and his pleasure in it." We may, of course, distinguish between morality and religion, between ethics and theology. As a matter of fact, however, moral laws have everywhere reposed upon the basis of religion, and their sanction has been sought in the principles of faith. As an immoral religion is false, so, if there is no God, a moral law is meaningless.

Theorists may be able to construct a system of ethics upon a foundation of materialism; but their mechanical and utilitarian doctrines have not the power to exalt the imagination or to confirm the will. Their educational value is feeble. Here in America we have already passed the stage of social development in which we might hold out to the young, as an ideal, the hope of becoming President of the Republic, or the possessor of millions of money. We know what sorry men presidents and millionnaires may be. We cannot look upon our country simply as a wide race-course with well-filled purses hanging at the goal for the prize-winners. We clearly perceive that a man's possessions are not himself, and that he is or ought to be more than anything which can belong to him. Ideals of excellence, therefore, must be substituted for those of success. Opinion governs the world, but ideals draw souls and stimulate to noble action. The more we transform with the aid of machinery the world of matter, the more necessary does it become that we make plain to all that man's true home is the world of thought and love, of hope and aspiration. The ideals of utilitarianism and secularism are unsatisfactory. They make no appeal to the infinite in man, to that in him which makes pursuit better than possession, and which, could he believe there is no absolute truth, love, and beauty, would lead him to despair. To-day, as of old, the soul is born of God and for God, and finds no peace unless it rest in him. Theology, assuredly, is not religion; but religion implies theology, and a church without a creed is a body without articulation. The virtues of religion are indispensable. Without them, it is not well either with individuals or with nations; but these virtues cannot be inculcated by those who, standing aloof from ecclesiastical organizations, are thereby cut off from the thought and work of all who in every age have most loved God, and whose faith in the soul has been most living. Religious men have wrought for God in the church, as patriots have wrought for liberty and justice in the nation; and to exclude the representatives of the churches from the school is practically to exclude religion,—the power which more than all others makes for righteousness, which inspires hope and confidence, which makes possible faith in the whole human brotherhood, in the face even of the political and social wrongs which are still everywhere tolerated. To exclude religion is to exclude the spirit of reverence, of gentleness and obedience, of modesty and purity; it is to exclude the spirit by which the barbarians have been civilized, by which woman has been uplifted and ennobled and the child made sacred. From many sides the demand is made that the State schools exercise a greater moral influence, that they be made efficient in forming character as well as in training the mind. It is recognized that knowing how to read and write does not insure good behavior. Since the State assumes the office of teacher, there is a disposition among parents to make the school responsible for their children's morals as well as for their minds, and thus the influence of the home is weakened. Whatever the causes may be, there seems to be a tendency, both in private and in public life, to lower ethical standards. The moral influence of the secular school is necessarily feeble, since our ideas of right and wrong are so interfused with the principles of Christianity that to ignore our religious convictions is practically to put aside the question of conscience. If the State may take no cognizance of sin, neither may its school do so. But in morals sin is the vital matter; crime is but its legal aspect. Men begin as sinners before they end as criminals.

The atmosphere of religion is the natural medium for the development of character. If we appeal to the sense of duty, we assume belief in God and in the freedom of the will; if we strive to awaken enthusiasm for the human brotherhood, we imply a divine fatherhood. Accordingly, as we accept or reject the doctrines of religion, the sphere of moral action, the nature of the distinction between right and wrong, and the motives of conduct all change. In the purely secular school only secular morality may be taught; and whatever our opinion of this system of ethics may otherwise be, it is manifestly deficient in the power which appeals to the heart and the conscience. The child lives in a world which imagination creates, where faith, hope, and love beckon to realms of beauty and delight. The spiritual and moral truths which are to become the very life-breath of his soul he apprehends mystically, not logically. Heaven lies about him; he lives in wonderland, and feels the thrill of awe as naturally as he looks with wide-open eyes. Do not seek to persuade him by telling him that honesty is the best policy, that poverty overtakes the drunkard, that lechery breeds disease, that to act for the common welfare is the surest way to get what is good for one's self; for such teaching will not only leave him unimpressed, but it will seem to him profane, and almost immoral. He wants to feel that he is the child of God, of the infinitely good and all-wonderful; that in his father, divine wisdom and strength are revealed; in his mother, divine tenderness and love. He so believes and trusts in God that it is our fault if he knows that men can be base. In nothing does the godlike character of Christ show forth more beautifully than in His reverence for children. Shall we profess to believe in Him, and yet forbid His name to be spoken in the houses where we seek to train the little ones whom He loved? Shall we shut out Him whose example has done more to humanize, ennoble, and uplift the race of man than all the teachings of the philosophers and all the disquisitions of the moralists? If the thinkers, from Plato and Aristotle to Kant and Pestalozzi, who have dealt with the problems of education, have held that virtue is its chief aim and end, shall we thrust from the school the one ideal character who, for nearly nineteen hundred years, has been the chief inspiration to righteousness and heroism; to whose words patriots and reformers have appealed in their struggles for liberty and right; to whose example philanthropists have looked in their labors to alleviate suffering; to whose teaching the modern age owes its faith in the brotherhood of men; by whose courage and sympathy the world has been made conscious that the distinction between man and woman is meant for the propagation of the race, but that as individuals they have equal rights and should have equal opportunities? We all, and especially the young, are influenced by example more than by precepts and maxims, and it is unjust and unreasonable to exclude from the schoolroom the living presence of the noblest and best men and women, of those whose words and deeds have created our Christian civilization. In the example of their lives we have truth and justice, goodness and greatness, in concrete form; and the young who are brought into contact with these centres of influence will be filled with admiration and enthusiasm; they will be made gentle and reverent; and they will learn to realize the ever-fresh charm and force of personal purity. Teachers who have no moral criteria, no ideals, no counsels of perfection, no devotion to God and godlike men, cannot educate, if the proper meaning of education is the complete unfolding of all man's powers.

The school, of course, is but one of the many agencies by which education is given. We are under the influence of our whole environment,—physical, moral, and intellectual; political, social, and religious; and if, in all this, aught were different, we ourselves should be other. The family is a school and the church is a school; and current American opinion assigns to them the business of moral and religious education. But this implies that conduct and character are of secondary importance; it supposes that the child may be made subject to opposite influences at home and in the school, and not thereby have his finer sense of reverence, truth, and goodness deadened. The subduing of the lower nature, of the outward to the inner man, is a thing so arduous that reason, religion, and law combined often fail to accomplish it. If one should propose to do away with schools altogether, and to leave education to the family and the Church, he would be justly considered ridiculous; because the carelessness of parents and the inability of the ministry of the Church would involve the prevalence of illiteracy. Now, to leave moral and religious education to the family and the churches involves, for similar reasons, the prevalence of indifference, sin, and crime. If illiteracy is a menace to free institutions, vice and irreligion are a greater menace. The corrupt are always bad citizens; the ignorant are not necessarily so. Parents who would not have their children taught to read and write, were there no free schools, will as a rule neglect their religious and moral education. In giving religious instruction to the young, the churches are plainly at a disadvantage; for they have the child but an hour or two in seven days, and they get into their Sunday classes only the children of the more devout.

If the chief end of education is virtue; if conduct is three-fourths of life; if character is indispensable, while knowledge is only useful,—then it follows that religion—which, more than any other vital influence, has power to create virtue, to inspire conduct, and to mould character—should enter into all the processes of education. Our school system, then, does not rest upon a philosophic view of life and education. We have done what it was easiest to do, not what it was best to do; and in this, as in other instances, churchmen have been willing to sacrifice the interests of the nation to the whims of a narrow and jealous temper. The denominational system of popular education is the right system. The secular system is a wrong system. The practical difficulties to be overcome that religious instruction may be given in the schools are relatively unimportant, and would be set aside if the people were thoroughly persuaded of its necessity. An objection which Dr. Harris, among others, insists upon, that the method of science and the method of religion are dissimilar, and that therefore secular knowledge and religious knowledge should not be taught in the same school, seems to me to have no weight. The method of mathematics is not the method of biology; the method of logic is not the method of poetry; but they are all taught in the same school. A good teacher, in fact, employs many methods. In teaching the child grammatical analysis, he has no fear of doing harm to his imagination or his talent for composition.

No system, however, can give assurance that the school is good. To determine this we must know the spirit which lives in it. The intellectual, moral, and religious atmosphere which the child breathes there is of far more importance, from an educational point of view, than any doctrines he may learn by rote, than any acts of worship he may perform.

The teacher makes the school; and when high, pure, devout, and enlightened men and women educate, the conditions favorable to mental and moral growth will be found, provided a false system does not compel them to assume a part and play a role, while the true self—the faith, hope, and love whereby they live—is condemned to inaction. The deeper tendency of the present age is not, I think, to exclude religion from any vital process, but rather to widen the content of the idea of religion until it embrace the whole life of man. The worship of God is not now the worship of infinite wisdom, holiness, and justice alone, but is also the worship of the humane, the beautiful, and the industriously active. Whether we work for knowledge or freedom, or purity or strength, or beauty or health, or aught else that is friendly to completeness of life, we work with God and for God. In the school, as in whatever other place in the boundless universe a man may find himself, he finds himself with God, in Him moves, lives, and has his being.

Chapter VII.

The Higher Education.[1]

The subject which I have been asked to treat is the higher education of priests; which, I suppose, is the highest education of man, since the ideal of the Christian priest is the most exalted, his vocation the most sublime, his office the most holy, his duties the most spiritual, and his mission—whether we consider its relation to morality, which is the basis of individual and social welfare, or to religion, which is the promise and the secret of immortal and godlike life—is the most important and the most sacred which can be assigned to a human being.

Religion and education—like religion and morality—are nearly related. Pure religion, indeed, is more than right education; and yet it may be said with truth that it is but a part of the best education, for it co-operates with other forces—with climate, custom, social conditions, and political institutions—to develop and fashion the complete man; and the special instruction of teachers—which is the narrow meaning of the word—is modified, and to a great extent controlled, by these powers which work unseen, and are the vital agents that make possible all conscious educational efforts.

The faith we hold, the laws we obey, the domestic and social customs to which our thoughts and loves are harmonized, the climate we live in, mould our characters and give to our souls a deeper and more lasting tinge than any school, though it were the best.

My subject, however, does not demand that I consider these general and silent agencies by which life is influenced, but leads me to the discussion

[1] A discourse pronounced at the Third Plenary Council of Baltimore, which, being enforced by the offer of three hundred thousand dollars by Miss Caldwell, led to the founding of the University at Washington.

of the methods by which man, with conscious purpose, seeks to form and instruct his fellow-man; to the discussion of the special education which brings art to the aid of nature, and becomes the auxiliary and guide of the other forces which contribute to the development of our being.

In this age, when all who think at all turn their thoughts to questions of education, it is needless to call attention to the interest of the subject, which, like hope, is immortal, and fresh as the innocent face of laughing childhood.

Is not the school for all men a shrine to which their pilgrim thoughts return to catch again the glow and gladness of a world wherein they lived by faith and hope and love when round the morning sun of life the golden purple clouds were hanging, and earth lay hidden in mist, beneath which the soul created a new paradise? To the opening mind all things are young and fair; and to remember the delight that accompanied the gradual dawn of knowledge upon our mental vision, sweet and beautiful as the upglowing of day from the bosom of night, is to be forever thankful for the gracious power of education. And is there not in all hearts a deep and abiding yearning for great and noble men, and therefore an imperishable interest in the power by which they are moulded? When fathers and mothers look upon the fair blossoming children that cling to them as the vine wraps its tendrils round the spreading bough, and when their great love fills them with ineffable longing to shield these tender souls from the blighting blasts of a cold and stormy world, and little by little to prepare them to stand alone and breast the gales of fortune, do they not instinctively put their trust in the power of education?

When, at the beginning of the present century, Germany lay prostrate at the feet of Napoleon, the wise and the patriotic among her children yielded not to despondency, but turned with confidence to truer methods and systems of education, and assiduous teaching and patient waiting finally brought them to Sedan.

When, in the sixteenth century, heresy and schism seemed near to final victory over the Church, Pope Julius III. declared that the evils and abuses of the times were the outgrowth of the shameful ignorance of the clergy, and that the chief hope of the dawning of a brighter day lay in general and thorough ecclesiastical education. And the Catholic leaders who finally turned back the advancing power of Protestantism, re-established the Church in half the countries in which it had been overthrown, and converted more souls in America and Asia than had been lost in Europe, belonged to the greatest educational body the world has ever seen. What is history but examples of success through knowledge and righteousness, and of failure through lack of understanding and of virtue?

Wherein lies the superiority of civilized races over barbarians if not in their greater knowledge and superior strength of character? And what but education has placed in the hands of man the thousand natural forces which he holds as a charioteer his well-reined steeds, bidding the winds carry him to distant lands, making steam his tireless, ever-ready slave, and commanding the lightning to speak his words to the ends of the earth? What else than this has taught him to map the boundless heavens, to read the footprints of God in the crust of the earth ages before human beings lived, to measure the speed of light, to weigh the imperceptible atom, to split up all natural compounds, to create innumerable artificial products with which he transforms the world and with a grain of powder marches like a conquering god around the globe?

What converts the meaningless babbling of the child into the stately march of oratoric phrase or the rhythmic flow of poetic language? What has developed the rude stone and bronze implements of savage and barbarous hordes into the miraculous machinery which we use? By what power has man been taught to carve the shapeless rock into an image of ideal beauty, or with it to build his thought into a temple of God, where the soul instinctively prostrates itself in adoration?

Is not all this, together with whatever else is excellent in human works, the result of education, which gives to man a second nature with more admirable endowments? And is not religion itself a kind of celestial education, which trains the soul to godlike life?

No progress in things divine or human is made by man except through effort, and effort is the power and the law of education. The maxim of the spiritual writers that not to struggle upward and onward is to be drawn downward, applies to every phase of our life. Whence do we derive strength of soul but from the uplifting of the mind and heart to God which we call prayer? To pray is to think, to attend, to hold the mind lovingly to its object; and this is what we do when we study. Hence prayer, which is the voice of religion, is a part of education,—nay, its very soul, breathing on all the chords of life, till their thousand dissonances meet in rhythmic harmony.

What is the pulpit but the holiest teacher's chair that has been placed upon the earth?

And as the presence of a noble character is a more potent influence than words, so sacramental communion with Christ is man's chief school of faith, of hope, and love. There are worthy persons who turn, as from an unholy thought, from the emphatic announcement of the need of the best human qualities for the proper defence of the cause of God in the world. Such speech seems to them to be vain and unreal; for God is all in all, and man is nothing. But in our day it is easier to go astray in the direction of self-annihilation than in that of self-assertion; since the common tendency now of all false philosophies is pantheistic, and issues in unconscious contempt of individual life. If man is but a bubble, merging forth and re-absorbed, without past or future, then indeed both he, and what he seems to do, sink into the eternal flow of matter, and are undeserving of a thought. This certainly is not the Christian view, to which man is revealed as a lesser god, and co-worker with the Eternal, whose thought can reach the infinite, and whose will can oppose that of the Omnipotent. In Christ, God co-operates with man for the salvation of the world; and in the Church, man co-operates with God to this same end. The more complete the man, the more fit is he to work with God. Even bodily disfigurement is looked upon as an obstacle; how much more, then, shall lack of intelligence and want of heart render us unworthy of the divine office? I certainly shall never deny that love, which the Apostle exalts above faith and hope, is higher also than knowledge. The light of the mind is as that of the moon—fair and soft and soothing, without heat, without the power to call forth and nourish life; but the light of the soul, which is love, is the sunlight, whose kiss, like a word of God, makes the dead to live, and clothes the world in strength and beauty. Character is more than intellect, love is more than knowledge, religion is more than morality; and a great heart brings us closer to God, nearer to all goodness, than a bright mind. Education is essentially moral, and the intellectual qualities themselves, which we seek to develop, derive their chief efficacy from underlying ethical qualities upon which they rest and from which they receive their energy and the power of self-control. Inequality of will is the great cause of inequality of mind; and the will is strengthened by the practice of virtue, as the body by food and exercise. If this is a general truth, with what special force must it not apply to the ministers of a religion the paramount and ceaseless aim of which is to make men holy, so that at times it has almost seemed as though the Church were indifferent as to whether they are learned or beautiful or strong? She pronounces no man a doctor unless he be also a saint; and when I insist that the priest shall possess the best mental culture of his age,—that without this he fights with broken weapons, speaks with harsh voice a language men will neither hear nor understand, teaches truths which, having not the freshness and the glow of truth, neither kindle the heart nor fire the imagination,—I do not forget that, without the moral earnestness which is born of faith and purity of life, mere cultivation of mind will not give him power to unseal the fountains of living waters which refresh the garden of God. The universal harmony is felt by a pure heart better than it can be perceived by a keen intellect. To a sinless soul the darker side even of life and nature is not wholly dark, and the mental difficulties which the existence of evil involves in no way weaken the consciousness of the essential goodness that lies at the heart of all things. In the religious, as in the moral world, men trust to what we are rather than to what we say, and the teacher of spiritual truth is never strong, unless his life and character inspire a confidence which arguments alone do not create; for in questions that reach beyond the sphere of sensation, we feel that insight is better than reasons, and hence we instinctively prefer the testimony of a god-like soul to the conclusions of a cultivated mind: and indeed our Blessed Lord ever assumes that the obstacle to the perception of divine truth is moral and not intellectual. The pure of heart see God; the evil-doer loves darkness and shuns the light. St. Paul goes even farther, and associates mental cultivation with a tendency directly opposed to religious faith, which is humble. "Knowledge puffeth up." But the words of the Apostle should not be stretched beyond his purpose, which is to point to pride as a special danger of the intellectual as sensuality is a danger of the ignorant. For man to have aught is to run a risk, and hence to do as little as possible is in the thought of the timid a mark of prudence. And indeed, if fear be nearer to wisdom than courage, then should we fear everything, for danger is everywhere. A breath may sow the seed of death; a look may slay the soul. In knowledge, in ignorance, in strength, in weakness, in wealth, in poverty, in genius, in stupidity, in company, in solitude, in innocence itself, danger lurks. But God does not abolish life that danger may cease to be; and they who put their trust in Him will not seek to darken the mind lest knowledge lead man astray, but will rather in a righteous cause make the venture of all things, as St. Ignatius preferred the hope of saving others to the certainty of his own salvation. And may we not maintain, since we hold that there is no inappeasable conflict between God and Nature, between the soul and matter, between revelation and science, that the apparent antagonism lies in our apprehension, and not in things themselves, and consequently that reconcilement is to be sought for through the help of thoroughly trained minds? The poet speaks the truth, "A little knowledge is a dangerous thing." They who know but little and imperfectly, see but their knowledge, if so it may be called, and walk in innocent unconsciousness of their infinite nescience. The narrower the range of our mental vision, the greater the obstinacy with which we cling to our opinions; and the half-educated, like the weak and the incompetent, are often contentious, but whosoever is able to do his work does it, and finds no time for dispute. He who possesses a disciplined mind, and is familiar with the best thoughts that live in the great literatures, will be the last to attach undue importance to his own thinking. A sense of decency and a kind of holy shame will keep him far from angry and unprofitable controversy; nor will he mistake a crotchet for a panacea, nor imagine that irritation is enlightenment. The blessings of a cultivated mind are akin to those of religion. They are larger liberty, wider life, purer delights, and a juster sense of the relative values of the means and ends which lie within our reach. Knowledge, like religion, leads us away from what appears to what is, from what passes to what remains, from what flatters the senses to that which speaks to the soul. Wisdom and religion converge, as love and knowledge meet in God; and to the wise as to the religious man, no great evil can happen. Into prison they both carry the sweet company of their thoughts, their faith and hope, and are freer in chains than the great in palaces. In death they are in the midst of life, for they see that what they know and love is imperishable, nor subject even to atomic disintegration. He who lives in the presence of truth yearns not for the company of men, but loves retirement as a saint loves solitude; and in times like ours, when men no longer choose the desert for a dwelling-place, the passionate desire of intellectual excellence co-operates with religious faith to guard them against dissipation and to lift them above the spirit of the age. The thinker is never lonely, as he who lives with God is never unhappy. Is not the love of excellence, which is the scholar's love, a part of the love of goodness which makes the saint? And are not intellectual delights akin to those religion brings? They are pure, they elevate, they refine; time only increases their charm, and in the winter of age, when the body is but the agent of pain, contemplation still remains like the light of a higher world, to tinge with beauty the clouds that gather around life's setting. How narrow and monotonous is sensation! how wide and various is thought! They who live in the senses are fettered and ill at ease; they who live in the soul are free and joyful. And since the priest, unless he be a saint, must have, like other men, some human joy, and since he dwells not in the sacred circle of the love of wife and children, in which the multitudes find repose and contentment, what solace, what refreshment, in the midst of cares and labors, shall we offer him? If there be aught for him that is not unworthy or dangerous, except the pleasures of the mind, to me it is unknown; and though a well-trained intellect should do no more than to enable us to take delight in pure and noble objects, it would be a chief help to worthy life. And when the whole tendency of our social existence is to draw men out of themselves and to make them seek the good of life in what is external, as money, display, position, renown, is it not a gain, if, while we open their minds to the charm of intellectual beauty, we make them see that this eager striving for wealth and place is a vulgar chase? And does not the spirit of refinement in thought, in speech, in manner, add worth and fairness to him whom it inspires, though the motive which preserves him from what is low or gross be no higher than a fastidious delicacy and self-respect?

To deny the moral influence of intellectual culture is as great an error as to affirm that it alone is a sufficient safeguard of morality. Its tendency unquestionably is to make men gentle, amiable, fair-minded, truthful, benevolent, modest, sober. It curbs ambition and teaches resignation; chastens the imagination and mitigates ferocity; dissuades from duelling because it is barbarous, and from war because it is cruel, and from persecution because it trusts in the prevalence of reason. It seeks to fit the mind and the character to the world, to all possible circumstances, so that whatever happens we remain ourselves,—calm, clear-seeing, able to do and to suffer. At great heights, or in the presence of irresistible force, as of a mighty waterfall, we grow dizzy; and in the same way, in the midst of multitudes, in the eagerness of strife, in the whirlwind of passion, equipoise is lost, and we cease to be ourselves, to become part of an aggregate of forces that hurry us on, whither we know not. To be able to stand in the presence of such power, and to feel its influence, and yet not to lose self-possession, is to be strong; is, on proper occasion, to be great. And the aim of the best education is to teach us the secret and the method of this complete self-control; and in so far it is not only moral, but also religious, though religion walks in a more royal road, and bids us love God and trust so absolutely in Him that life and death become equal, and all the ways and workings of men as the storm to one who on lofty mountain peak, amid the blue heavens, with the sunlight around him and the quiet breathing of the winds, sees far below, as in another world, the black clouds and lurid lightning flash and hears the roll of distant thunder.

It is far from my thought, it is needless to say, that mental cultivation can be made to take the place or do the work of religion, even in the case of the very few for whom the best discipline of mind is possible. My aim is simply to show that the type of character which it tends to create is not necessarily at variance with religious principle and life, as is, for instance, that of the mere worldling; but that it conspires with Christian faith to produce, if not the same, at least similar virtues, though its ethical influence is comparatively superficial, and the moral qualities which it produces lack consistency and the power to withstand the fire of the passions. It is enough for my purpose to point out that if intellectualism is often the foe of religious truth, there is no good reason why it should not also be its ally.

No excellence, as I conceive, of whatever kind, is rejected by Catholic teaching, and the perfection of the mind is not less divine than the perfection of the heart. It is good to know, as it is good to hope, to believe, to love. A cultivated intellect, an open mind, a rich imagination, with correctness of thought, flexibility of view, and eloquent expression, are among the noblest endowments of man; and though they should serve no other purpose than to embellish life, to make it fairer and freer, they would nevertheless be possessions without price, for the most nobly useful things are those which make life good and beautiful. Like virtue they are their own reward, and like mercy they bear a double blessing. It is the fashion with many to affect contempt for men of superior culture, because they look upon education as simply a means to tangible ends, and think knowledge valuable only when it can be made to serve practical purposes. This is a narrow and a false view; for all men need the noble and the beautiful, and he who lives without an ideal is hardly a man. Our material wants are not the most real for being the most sensible and pressing, and they who create or preserve for us models of spiritual and intellectual excellence are our greatest benefactors. Which were the greater loss for England, to be without Wellington and Nelson, or to be without Shakspeare and Milton? Whatever the answer be, in the one case England would suffer, in the other the whole world would feel the loss. Though a thoroughly trained intellect is less worthy of admiration than a noble character, its power is immeasurably greater; for, example can influence but a few and for a short time, but when a truth or a sentiment has once found its best expression, it becomes a part of literature, and like a proverb is current forevermore; and so the kings of thought become immortal rulers, and without their help the godlike deeds of saints and heroes would be buried in oblivion. "Words pass," said Napoleon, "but deeds remain." The man of action exaggerates the worth of action, but the philosopher knows that to act is easy, to think, difficult; and that great deeds spring from great thoughts. There are words that never grow silent, there are words that have changed the face of the earth, and the warrior's wreath of victory is entwined by the Muse's hand. The power of Athens is gone, her temples are in ruins, the Acropolis is discrowned, and from Mars' Hill no voice thunders now; but the words of Socrates, the great deliverer of the mind, and the father of intellectual culture, still breathe in the thoughts of every cultivated man on earth. The glory of Jerusalem has departed, the broken stones of Solomon's Temple lie hard by the graves that line the brook of Kedron, and from the minaret of Mount Sion the misbeliever's melancholy call sounds like a wail over a lost world; but the songs of David still rise from the whole earth in heavenly concert, upbearing to the throne of God the faith and hope and love of countless millions. And is not the Blessed Saviour the Eternal Word? And is not the Bible God's word? And is not the Gospel the Word, which, like an electric thrill, runs to the ends of the world? "Currit verbum," says St. Paul. "Man lives not on bread alone, but on every word that cometh forth from the mouth of God." Nay, there is life in all the true and noble thoughts that have blossomed in the mind of genius and filled the earth with fragrance and with fruit.

Shall I be told that the intellectual cultivation and discipline, which gives to man control of his knowledge, the perfect use of his faculties, justness of perception with ease and grace of expression, cannot bring serviceable advocacy or defence to the cause of divine truth? What does truth need but to be known? And since to reach the mind and heart of man it must be clothed in words, what is so necessary to it as the garb and vesture, the form and color, the warmth and life, which shall so mark it that to be loved it needs but be seen? And who shall so clothe it, if not he who has the freest, the most flexible, the clearest, the best disciplined mind? In the apostolic age, when the manifestations of miraculous power accompanied the announcement of Christian doctrine, the lack of the persuasive words of human eloquence was not felt. Let him who can drink poison and touch scorpions, and not suffer harm, despise the aid of learning; but for us, who are not so assisted, no cultivation of mind or preparation of heart can be too great; and to appear in the garb of a savage were less unseemly than to speak the holiest and the highest truths in the barbarous tongue of ignorance.

Our way here cannot be doubtful. Either we must hold with certain peculiar heretics that learning is a hindrance to the efficacious teaching of religious truth, or, denying this, we must hold, since mental culture is serviceable, that the best is most serviceable.

May we not take this for a principle,—to believe that God does everything, and then to act as though He left everything for us to do? Or this: Since grace supposes nature, the growth and strength of the Church is not wholly independent of the natural endowments of her ministers?

As a matter of fact we Catholics are constantly speaking and acting upon principles of this kind. We maintain that without a proper education our children must lose the faith; and that without careful moral and mental training no man is likely to become a good priest; and all that I further insist upon is that if he is to do the best work, he must have the best intellectual discipline. In an intellectual age, at least, he cannot be the worthy minister of worship, unless he is also the accomplished teacher of truth. In vain shall we clothe him in rich symbolic vestments, place him in majestic temples, before marble altars, in the midst of solemn music, in the dim sober-tinted light, with the great and noble looking out upon him, as from a spirit world,—in vain shall all this be, if when he himself speaks, his words are felt to be but the echo of a coarse and empty mind. And hence our enemies would gladly leave us the poetry of our worship, would even enter our churches to be comforted, to be soothed, to seek the elevation and enlargement of thought and sentiment which comes upon us in the presence of what is vast, mysterious, and sublime, if we would but confess that it is only poetry, good and beautiful only as art is good and beautiful. The spirit of the time, in fact, it seems to me, is more and more disposed to grant us everything except the possession of intellectual truth. That the Catholic Church is a marvellous power; that her triumphs have been so enduring and so unexpected that only the foolish or the ignorant will predict her downfall; that she overcame paganism; that she saved Christianity when Rome fell; that she restrained the ferocity of the barbarians, protected the weak, encouraged labor, preserved the classics, maintained the unity and sanctity of marriage, defended the purity and dignity of woman, espoused the cause of the oppressed, and in a lawless and ignorant age proclaimed the supremacy of right and the worth of learning; that to these signal services must be added her power to give ease and pleasantness to the social relations of men, keeping them equally remote from Puritan severity and pagan license; her eye for beauty and grace, which has made her the foster-mother of all the arts; her love of the excellent and the noble, which has enabled her to create types of character that are immortal; her practical wisdom, giving her the secret of dealing with every phase of life, so that her saints are doctors, apostles, mystics, philanthropists, artists, poets, kings, beggars, warriors, peasants, barbarians, philosophers,—all this, if I mistake not, unbelievers even are more and more willing to concede. Nor are they slow to express their admiration of the strength and majesty of this single power amid the Christian nations, which reaches back to the great civilizations that have perished, which has preserved its organic unity intact amid the social revolutions of two thousand years, and which is acknowledged still to be the greatest moral force in the world. But, underlying all they say and think, is the assumption that the foundations of this noble structure are crumbling; that the world of faith and thought in which it was upbuilt is become a desert where no flower blooms, no living soul is found; that the temple is beautiful only as a ruin is beautiful, where owls hoot and bats flit to and fro. "There is not a creed, we are told, which is not shaken, nor an accredited dogma which is not shown to be questionable; not a received tradition which does not threaten to dissolve."

The conquests of the human mind in the realms of nature have produced a world-wide ferment of thought, an intellectual activity which is without a parallel. They have increased the power of man to an almost incredible degree, have given him control of the earth and the seas, have placed within his grasp undreamed-of forces, have opened to his view unsuspected mysteries; they have placed him on a new earth and under new heavens, and thrown a light never seen before upon the history of his race. As a part of this vast development new questions have risen, new theories have been broached, new doubts have suggested themselves; and because we have changed, all else seems to have changed also. And since, underlying all questions, there is found a question of religion, the discussion of religious and philosophic problems has, in our day, become a social necessity, and the science of criticism, together with the physical sciences, has driven the disputants upon new and difficult ground, where the battle must be fought, and where retreat is not possible.

As well imagine that society will again take on the form of feudalism, as that the human mind will return to the point of view from which our ancestors looked on nature.

And this world-view shapes and colors all our thinking, in theology as in other sciences, so that truths which were latent have come to light, and principles which have long been held find new and wider application.

Never has the defence of religion required so many and such excellent qualities of intellect as in the present day. The early apologists who contrasted the sublimity and purity of Christian faith with a corrupt paganism had not a difficult task. In the Middle Age the intellect of the world was on the side of Christ. The controversy which sprang up with the advent of Protestantism was biblical and historical, and its criticism was superficial. The anti-Christian schools of thought of the eighteenth century were literary rather than philosophical, and the objections they urged were founded chiefly upon political and social considerations. In all these discussions the territory in dispute was well defined and relatively small. But into what a different world are not we thrown! These earlier explorers sailed upon rivers whose banks were lined by firm-set rocky cliffs, by the overshadowing boughs of primeval forests, with here and there pleasant slopes of green where they might lie at rest amid the fragrance of wild flowers; but from our Peter's bark we look out upon the dark unfathomed seas towards an unknown world whose margin ever fades and recedes as we seem to draw near the haven of our desire.

As in the beginning of the twelfth century the cry, "God wills it!" rang through Europe, and from all her lands armies of mailed knights sprang into battle-array and turned their faces towards the Holy City, resolved to wrench from infidel hands the Sacred Tomb of Christ, so now, from her thousand watch-towers, science sounds her clarion note with quite other intent, urging on to the attack of the citadel of God in the heart of man, renewing upon lower fields the war in which immortal spirits contended with the Almighty "in dubious battle on the plains of heaven, and shook his throne." As "he jests at scars that never felt a wound," so here the lesser knowledge makes the bolder man. Not that difficulties should create doubts, or that objections may not be answered, or that it is necessary to refute each hypothesis that appears and fades like a dissolving view, or to notice each unwarrantable inference from unquestioned facts, or that it is worth while to address ourselves to minds whose nebulous and shifting opinions make it impossible that they should receive correct impressions; but the field upon which attacks upon religion are now made is so vast, the confusion of thought into which new discoveries and speculations have thrown the minds of even educated men is so bewildering, the methods for the ascertainment of truth are so tangled and misapplied, the rushing on of multitudes to discuss problems which have hitherto been left to philosophers, and which they alone can rightly enunciate, is so stupefying, that those who have the clearest perception of the mental state of the modern world, and who are able to take the finest and most comprehensive view of the religious, philosophic, and scientific controversies of the day, seem loath to enter into a struggle where the ground continually changes, and where victory at the best is only partial, and but leads to further contest. It is well to remember, also, that in the intellectual arena to attack is easier than to defend, and any shallow, incoherent talker or writer can propose difficulties which the keenest thinker will find great trouble to explain. Since we and our works fall to ruin and pass away, we seem instinctively to take the side of those who seek to undermine and overthrow systems of thought and belief which claim to be indestructible, and the human heart is half a traitor to the Church which declares that she is indefectible and infallible. Is there not indeed, however we account for it, in all nature a kind of dread and horror of the supernatural, such as one who hides within his bosom a secret of dark guilt feels in the presence of the conscience of mankind? And does not this make the world lean to the side of those who would eliminate God from nature?

And yet, since man's heart is the home of contradictions, is it not also true to say that he is naturally religious? His faith in God is as deep and unwavering as his faith in the testimony of the senses; and if there are atheists there are also men who hold that all things are unreal and only appear to be; that the world is but a myriad-formed, a myriad-tinted idea, the dream of a substanceless dreamer. Not only do we believe in God and in the soul, but all that we love, all that we hope for, all that gives to life charm, dignity, and sacredness, is interpenetrated, perfumed, and illumined by this faith. If men could be persuaded that the unconscious is the beginning and the end of all things, what good would have been gained? The light of heaven would fade away, and the soul's high faith be made a lie; the poor would have no friend, and the rich no heart; the wicked would be without fear, and the good without hope; success would be consecrated, and death alone would remain as the refuge of the unfortunate. Even animal indulgence, in sinking out of the moral order, would lose its human charm. If then in our day there is wide-spread scepticism, a sort of vague feeling that science is undermining religion and that the most sacred beliefs are dissolving, the cause of this lies not so much in the natural tendencies of the mind and heart, as in social conditions, in passing phases of thought, in the shifting of the point of view from which men have hitherto been accustomed to look on nature; and the continuance and the progress of doubt, and consequently of indifference, is, to some extent at least, to be ascribed also to the fact that the most earnest believers in God and in Christianity have, for now more than a century, been less eager to acquire the best philosophic and literary cultivation of mind than others who, having lost faith in the supernatural, seek for compensation in a wider and deeper knowledge of nature, and in the mental culture which enables them to enjoy more keenly the high thoughts and fair images which live in literature and art. As a well-trained intellect, in argument with the unskilful, easily makes the worse appear the better cause, so in an age or a country where the best discipline of mind is found chiefly among those who are not Christians, or at least not Catholics, public opinion will drift away from the Church, until the view finally becomes general that, whatever she may have been in other times, her day is past. Nor will aught external, however fair or glorious, secure her against this danger. How often in the history of nations and of religions is not outward splendor the mark of inward decay? When Rome was free, a simple life sufficed; but when liberty fled, marble palaces arose. The monarch who built Versailles made the scaffold on which French royalty perished; and so a dying faith, like the setting sun, may drape itself in glory. The Kingdom of God is within; there is the source of life and strength, without which nor numbers nor wealth, nor stately edifices nor solemn rites, avail. Nor can we be certain of men's love when we cease to have influence over their thoughts. The proper appeal is to the heart through the mind; and even a mother loses half her power when she ceases to be the intellectual superior of her children. How then shall the heavenly Mother of the soul keep her place in the world, if those who speak in her name mar by imperfect and ignorant utterance the celestial harmony of her doctrines?

Ah! let us learn to see things as they are. In face of the modern world, that which the Catholic priest most needs, after virtue, is the best cultivation of mind, which issues in comprehensiveness of view, in exactness of perception, in the clear discernment of the relations of truths and of the limitations of scientific knowledge, in fairness and flexibility of thought, in ease and grace of expression, in candor, in reasonableness; the intellectual culture which brings the mind into form gives it the control of its faculties, creates the habit of attention, and develops firmness of grasp. The education of which I speak is expansion and discipline of mind rather than learning; and its tendency is not so much to form profound dogmatists, or erudite canonists, or acute casuists, as to cultivate a habit of mind, which, for want of a better word, may be called philosophical; to enlarge the intellect, to strengthen and supple its faculties, to enable it to take connected views of things and their relations, and to see clear amid the mazes of human error and through the mists of human passion. I speak of that perfection of the intellect, which, to use the words of Cardinal Newman, "is the clear, calm, accurate vision and comprehension of all things as far as the finite mind can embrace them, each in its place and with its own characteristics upon it. It is almost prophetic from its knowledge of history; it is almost heart-searching from its knowledge of human nature; it has almost supernatural charity from its freedom from littleness and prejudice; it has almost the repose of faith because nothing can startle it; it has almost the beauty and harmony of heavenly contemplation, so intimate is it with the eternal order of things and the music of the spheres." This is, indeed, ideal; but they who believe not in ideals were not born to know the real worth of things:

"Spite of proudest boast
Reason, best reason is to imperfect man
An effort only and a noble aim,—
A crown, an attribute of sovereign power,
Still to be courted, never to be won."

It is plain that education of this kind aims at something quite different from the mere imparting of useful knowledge. It takes the view that it is good to know, even though knowledge should not be a means to wealth or power or any other common aim of life. It regards the mind as the organ of truth, and trains it for its own sake, without reference to the exercise of a profession. Hence its distinguishing characteristic is that it is liberal and not professional. It holds cultivated faculties in higher esteem than learning, and it makes use of knowledge to improve the intellect, rather than of the intellect to acquire knowledge. Hence, one may be a skilful physician, a judicious lawyer, a learned theologian, and yet be greatly lacking in mental culture. It is a common experience to find that professional men are apt to be narrow and one-sided. Their mind, like the dyer's hand, is subdued to what it works in. They want comprehensiveness of view, flexibility of thought, openness to light, and freedom of mental play. They think in grooves, make the rules of their art the measure of truth, and their own methods of inquiry the only valid laws of reasoning. These same defects may be observed in those who are given exclusively to the study of physical science. When they sweep the heavens with the telescope and do not find God, they conclude that there is no God. When the soul does not reveal itself under the microscope, they argue it does not exist; and since there is no thought without nervous movement, they claim that the brain thinks.

Now, if it is desirable that those who are charged with the teaching and defence of divine truth should be free from this narrowness and one-sidedness, this lack of openness to light and freedom of mental play, the education of the priest must be more than a professional education; and he must be sent to a school higher and broader than the ecclesiastical seminary, which is simply a training college for the practical work of the ministry. The purpose for which it was instituted is to prepare young men for the worthy exercise of the general functions of the priestly office, and the good it has done is too great and too manifest to need commendation. But the ecclesiastical seminary is not a school of intellectual culture, either here in America or elsewhere, and to imagine that it can become the instrument of intellectual culture is to cherish a delusion. It must impart a certain amount of professional knowledge, fit its students to become more or less expert catechists, rubricists, and casuists, and its aim is to do this; and whatever mental improvement, if any, thence results, is accidental. Hence its methods are not such as one would choose who desires to open the mind, to give it breadth, flexibility, strength, refinement, and grace. Its text-books are written often in a barbarous style, the subjects are discussed in a dry and mechanical way, and the professor, wholly intent upon giving instruction, is frequently indifferent as to the manner in which it is imparted; or else not possessing himself a really cultivated intellect, he holds in slight esteem expansion and refinement of mind, looking upon it as at the best a mere ornament. I am not offering a criticism upon the ecclesiastical seminary, but am simply pointing to the plain fact that it is not a school of intellectual culture, and consequently, if its course were lengthened to five, to six, to eight, to ten years, its students would go forth to their work with a more thorough professional training, but not with more really cultivated minds. The test of intellect is not so much what we know as the manner in which it is known; just as in the moral world, the important consideration is not what virtues we possess, but the completeness with which they are ours. He who really believes in God, serves Him, loves Him, is a hero, a saint; whereas he who half believes may have a thousand good qualities, but not a great character. Knowledge is not education any more than food is nutrition; and as one may eat voraciously, and yet remain without bodily health or strength, so one may have great learning, and yet be almost wholly lacking in intellectual cultivation. His learning may only oppress and confuse him, be felt as a load, and not as a vital principle, which upraises, illumines, and beautifies the mind; mentally he may still be a boy, in whom memory predominates, and whose intellect is only a receptacle of facts. Memory is the least noble of the intellectual faculties, and the nearest to animal intelligence; and to know well is, in the eyes of a true educator, of quite other importance than to know much. But a memory, more or less well-stored, is nearly all a youth carries with him from the college to the seminary, and here he enters, as I have already pointed out, upon a course not of intellectual discipline, but of professional studies, whose object is not "to open the mind, to correct it, to refine it, to enable it to know, and to digest, master, rule, and use its knowledge, to give it power over its own faculties, application, flexibility, method, critical exactness, sagacity, resource, eloquent expression," but simply to impart the requisite skill for the ordinary exercise of the holy ministry. Hence it is not surprising that priests who are zealous, earnest, self-sacrificing, who to piety join discretion and good sense, rarely possess the intellectual culture of which I am speaking, for the simple reason that a university and not a seminary is the school in which this kind of education is received. That the absence of such trained intellects is a most serious obstacle to the progress of the Catholic faith, no thoughtful man will doubt or deny. Since the mind is a power, in religion, as in every sphere of thought and life, the discipline which best develops and perfects its faculties will fit it to do its work, whatever it may be, in the most effective manner. Hence, though the education of which I speak does not directly aim at being useful, it is in fact the most useful, and prepares better than any other for the business of life. It enables a man to master a subject with ease, to fill an office with honor; and whatever he does, the mark of completeness and finish will be found upon his work. He sees more clearly, judges more calmly, reasons more pertinently, speaks more seasonably than other men. The free and full possession of his faculties gives him power to turn himself to whatever may be demanded of him, whether it be to govern wisely, or to counsel judiciously, or to write gracefully, or to plead eloquently. Whatever course in life he may take, whatever line of thought or investigation he may pursue, his intellectual culture will give him superiority over men who, with equal or greater talents, lack his education; and he possesses withal resources within himself, which in a measure make him independent of fortune, and which, when failure comes and the world abandons him, remain, like faith, or hope, or a friend, to make him forget his misfortunes.

Of the English universities, with all their shortcomings, Cardinal Newman says: "At least they can boast of a succession of heroes and statesmen, of literary men and philosophers, of men conspicuous for great natural virtues, for habits of business, for knowledge of life, for practical judgment, for cultivated tastes, for accomplishments, who have made England what it is,—able to subdue the earth, able to domineer over Catholics." It is only in a university that all the sciences are brought together, their relations adjusted, their provinces assigned. There natural science is limited by metaphysics; morality is studied in the light of history; language and literature are viewed from the standpoint of ethnology; the criticism which seeks beauty and not deformity, which in the gardens of the mind takes the honey and leaves the poison, is applied to the study of eloquence and poetry; and over all religion throws the warmth and life of faith and hope, like a ray from heaven. The mind thus lives in an atmosphere in which the comparison of ideas and truths with one an other is inevitable; and so it grows, is strengthened, enlarged, refined, made pliant, candid, open, equitable.

When numbers of priests will be able to bring this cultivation of intellect to the treatment of religious subjects, then will Catholic theology again come forth from its isolation in the modern world; then will Catholic truth again irradiate and perfume the thoughts and opinions of men; then will Catholic doctrines again sink into their hearts, and not remain loose in the mind to be thrown aside, as one casts away the outworn vesture of the body; then will it be felt that the fascination of Christian faith is still fresh, supreme, as far above the charm of science as the joy of a poet's soul is above the pleasures of sense. The religious view of life must forever remain the true view, since no other explains our longings and aspirations, or justifies hope and enthusiasm; and the worship of God in spirit and in truth, which Christ has revealed to the world, the religion not of an age or a people, but of all time and of the human race, must eternally prevail when brought home to us in a language which we understand; for we place the testimony of reason above that of the senses. To the eye the sun rises and sets, to the mind it is stationary; and we accept, not what is seen, but what is known.

Is there need of stronger evidence that the power within, which is our real self, is spiritual? And is it not enough to see clearly, to perceive that in the struggle of mind with matter, which is the essential form of the conflict of spiritualism with materialism, of religion with science, the soul, in the end, will be victorious, and rest in the real world of faith and intuition, and not in the pictured world of the senses?

Religion, indeed, like morality, is in the nature of things, and Catholic faith is Una's Red Cross Knight, on whose shield are old dints of deep wounds and cruel marks of many a bloody field, who is assailed by all the powers of earth and of the nether world, armed with whatever weapons may hurt the mind or corrupt the heart, but whom heavenly Providence rescues from the jaws of monsters and leads on to victory.

But what true believer thinks himself excused from effort, because Christ has declared that the gates of hell shall not prevail against His Church? Does he not know that though, when we consider her whole course through the world, she has triumphed, so as to have become the miracle of history, yet has she at many points suffered disastrous defeat? Hence, those who love her must be vigilant, and stand prepared for battle. And in an age when persecution has either died away or lost its harshness, when crying abuses have disappeared, when heresy has run its course, and the struggle of the world with the Church has become almost wholly intellectual, it is not possible, assuredly, that her ministers should have too great power of intellect. And consequently it is not possible that the bishops, in whose hands the education of priests is placed, should have too great a care that they receive the best mental culture. And if this is a general truth, with what pertinency does it not come home to us here in America, who are the descendants of men who, on account of their faith, have for centuries been oppressed and thrust back from opportunities of education, and who, when persecution and robbery had reduced them to ignorance and poverty, were forced to hear their religion reproached with the crimes of her foes? And now, when at length a fairer day has dawned for us in this new world, what can be more natural than our eager desire to move out from the valleys of darkness towards the hills and mountain tops that are bathed in sunlight? What more praiseworthy than the fixed resolve to prove that not our faith, but our misfortunes made and kept us inferior. And, since we live in the midst of millions who have indeed good will towards us, but who still bear the yoke of inherited prejudices, and who, because for three hundred years real cultivation of mind was denied to Catholics who spoke English, conclude that Protestantism is the source of enlightenment, and the Church the mother of ignorance, do not all generous impulses urge us to make this reproach henceforth meaningless? And in what way shall we best accomplish this task? Surely not by writing or speaking about what the influence of the Church is, or by pointing to what she has done in other ages, but by becoming what we claim her spirit tends to make us. Here, if anywhere, the proverb is applicable—*verba movent, exempla trahunt*. As the devotion of American Catholics to this country and its free institutions, as shown not on battle-fields alone, but in our whole bearing and conduct, convinces all but the unreasonable of the depth and sincerity of our patriotism, so when our zeal for intellectual excellence shall have raised up men who will take place among the first writers and thinkers of their day their very presence will become the most persuasive of arguments to teach the world that no best gift is at war with the spirit of Catholic faith, and that, while the humblest mind may feel its force, the lofty genius of Augustine, of Dante, and of Bossuet is upborne and strengthened by the splendor of its truth. But if we are to be intellectually the equals of others, we must have with them equal advantages of education; and so long as we look rather to the multiplying of schools and seminaries than to the creation of a real university, our progress will be slow and uncertain, because a university is the great ordinary means to the best cultivation of mind. The fact that the growth of the Church here, like that of the country itself, is chiefly external, a growth in wealth and in numbers, makes it the more necessary that we bring the most strenuous efforts to improve the gifts of the soul. The whole tendency of our social life insures the increase of churches, convents, schools, hospitals, and asylums; our advance in population and in wealth will be counted from decade to decade by millions, and our worship will approach more and more to the pomp and splendor of the full ritual; but this very growth makes such demands upon our energies, that we are in danger of forgetting higher things, or at least of thinking them less urgent. Few men are at once thoughtful and active. The man of deeds dwells in the world around him; the thinker lives within his mind. Contemplation, in widening the view, makes us feel that what even the strongest can do is lost in the limitless expanse of space and time; and the soul is tempted to fall back upon itself and to gaze passively upon the course of the world, as though the general stream of human events were as little subject to man's control as the procession of the seasons. Busy workers, on the other hand, having little taste or time for reflection, see but the present and what lies close to them, and the energy of their doing circumscribes their thinking.

But the Church needs both the men who act and the men who think; and since with us everything pushes to action, wisdom demands that we cultivate rather the powers of reflection. And this is the duty alike of true patriots and of faithful Catholics. All are working to develop our boundless material resources; let a few at least labor to develop man. The millions are building cities, reclaiming wildernesses, and bringing forth from the earth its buried treasures; let at least a remnant cherish the ideal, cultivate the beautiful, and seek to inspire the love of moral and intellectual excellence. And since we believe that the Church which points to heaven is able also to lead the nations in the way of civilization and of progress, why should we not desire to see her become a beneficent and ennobling influence in the public life of our country? She can have no higher temporal mission than to be the friend of this great republic, which is God's best earthly gift to His children. If, as English critics complain, our style is inflated, it is because we feel the promise of a destiny which transcends our powers of expression. Whatever fault men may find with us, let them not doubt the world-wide significance of our life. If we keep ourselves strong and pure, all the peoples of the earth shall yet be free; if we fulfil our providential mission, national hatred shall give place to the spirit of generous rivalry, the people shall become wiser and stronger, society shall grow more merciful and just, and the cry of distress shall be felt, like the throb of a brother's heart, to the ends of the world. Where is the man who does not feel a kind of religious gratitude as he looks upon the rise and progress of this nation? Above all, where is the Catholic whose heart is not enlarged by such contemplation? Here, almost for the first time in her history, the Church is really free. Her worldly position does not overshadow her spiritual office, and the State recognizes her autonomy. The monuments of her past glory, wrenched from her control, stand not here to point, like mocking fingers, to what she has lost. She renews her youth, and lifts her brow, as one who, not unmindful of the solemn mighty past, yet looks with undimmed eye and unfaltering heart to a still more glorious future. Who in such a presence, can abate hope, or give heed to despondent counsel, or send regretful thoughts to other days and lands? Whoever at any time, in any place, might have been sage, saint, or hero, may be so here and now; and though he had the heart of Francis, and the mind of Augustine, and the courage of Hildebrand, here is work for him to do.

In whatsoever direction we turn our thoughts, arguments rush in to show the pressing need for us of a centre of life and light such as a Catholic university would be. Without this we can have no hope of entering as a determining force into the living controversies of the age; without this it must be an accident if we are represented at all in the literature of our country; without this we shall lack a point of union to gather up, harmonize, and intensify our scattered forces; without this our bishops must remain separated, and continue to work in random ways; without this the noblest souls will look in vain for something larger and broader than a local charity to make appeal to their generous hearts; without this we shall be able to offer but feeble resistance to the false theories and systems of education which deny to the Church a place in the school; without this the sons of wealthy Catholics will, in ever increasing numbers, be sent to institutions where their faith is undermined; without this we shall vainly hope for such treatment of religious questions and their relations to the issues and needs of the day, as shall arrest public attention and induce Catholics themselves to take at least some little notice of the writings of Catholics; without this in struggles for reform and contests for rights we shall lack the wisdom of best counsel and the courage which skilful leaders inspire. We are a small minority in the presence of a vast majority; we still bear the disfigurements and weaknesses of centuries of persecution and suffering; we cling to an ancient faith in an age when new sciences, discoveries, and theories fascinate the minds of men, and turn their thoughts away from the past to the future; we preach a spiritual religion to a people whose prodigious wealth and rapid triumphs over nature have caused them to exaggerate the value of material progress; we teach the duty of self-denial to a refined and intellectual generation, who regard whatever is painful as evil, whatever is difficult as omissible; we insist upon religious obedience to the Church in face of a society where children are ceasing to reverence and obey even their parents;—if in spite of all this we are to hold our own, not to speak of larger hopes, it is plain that we may neglect nothing which will help us to put forth our full strength.

I do not, of course, pretend that this higher education is all that we need, or that, of itself, it is sufficient; but what I claim is that it would be a source of strength for us who are in want of help. God works in many ways, through many agencies, and I bow in homage to the humblest effort in a righteous cause of the lowliest human being. There are diversities of graces, but the same spirit; diversities of ministries, but the same Lord. *Numquid omnes doctores?* asks St. Paul. But since he places teachers by the side of apostles and prophets, surely they will teach to best purpose who to the humility of faith add the luminousness of knowledge. To those who reject the idea of human co-operation in things divine I speak not; but we who believe that we are co-operators with Christ cannot think that it is possible to bring to this godlike work either too great preparation of heart or too great cultivation of mind. Nor must we think lightly even of refinement of thought and speech and behavior, for we know that manners come of morals, and that morals in turn are born of manners, as the ocean breathes forth the clouds and the clouds fill the ocean.

Let there be then an American Catholic university, where our young men, in the atmosphere of faith and purity, of high thinking and plain living, shall become more intimately conscious of the truth of their religion and of the genius of their country; where they shall learn the repose and dignity which belong to their ancient Catholic descent, and yet not lose the fire which glows in the blood of a new people; to which from every part of the land our eyes may turn for guidance and encouragement, seeking light and self-confidence from men in whom intellectual power is not separate from moral purpose, who look to God and His universe from bending knees of prayer, who uphold—

> "The cause of Christ and civil liberty
> As one, and moving to one glorious end."

Should such an intellectual centre serve no other purpose than to bring together a number of eager-hearted, truth-loving youths, what light and heat would not leap forth from the shock of mind with mind; what generous rivalries would not spring up; what intellectual sympathies, resting on the breast of faith, would not become manifest, grouping souls like atoms, to form the substance and beauty of a world?

O solemn groves that lie close to Louvain and to Freiburg, whose air is balm and whose murmuring winds sound like the voices of saints and sages whispering down the galleries of time, what words have ye not heard bursting forth from the strong hearts of keen-witted youths, who, Titan-like, believed they might storm the citadel of God's truth! How many a one, heavy and despondent, in the narrow, lonesome path of duty, has remembered you, and moved again in unseen worlds, upheld by faith and hope! Who has listened to the words of your teachers and not felt the truth of the saying of Pope Pius II.,—that the world holds nothing more precious or more beautiful than a cultivated intellect? The presence of such men invigorates like mountain air, and their speech is as refreshing as clear-flowing fountains. To know them is to be forever their debtor. The company of a saint is the school of saints; a strong character develops strength in others, and a noble mind makes all around him luminous.

Why may not eight million Catholics upbuild a home for great teachers, for men who, to real learning and cultivation of mind, shall add the persuasiveness of easy and eloquent diction; whose manifest and indisputable superiority shall put to shame the self-conceit of American young men, our most familiar intellectual bane, and an insuperable obstacle to all improvement,—self-conceit, which is the beatitude of vulgar characters and shallow minds? If our students should find in such an institution but one man, who, like Socrates, with ironic questioning might make for them the discovery of the new world of their own ignorance, the gain would be great enough.

Why may we not have a centre of light and truth which will raise up before us standards of intellectual excellence; which will enable us to see that our so-called educated men are as far from being scholars as the makers of our horrible show-bills are from being artists; which will teach us that it is not only false but vulgar to call things by pretentious names,—as, for instance, to call a politician a statesman, a declaimer an orator, or a Latin school a university.

Ah! surely as to whether an American Catholic university is desirable there cannot be two opinions among enlightened men. But is it feasible? A true university is one of the noblest foundations of the great Catholic ages, when faith rose almost to the height of creative power, and it were folly in me to maintain that such an undertaking is not surrounded by many and great difficulties. To begin with the material for foundation, money is necessary, and this, I am persuaded, we may have. A noble cause will find or make generous hearts. Men above all we need, for every kind of existence propagates itself only by itself. But let us bear in mind that the best teacher is not necessarily or often he who knows the most, but he who has most power to determine the student to self-activity; for in the end the mind educates itself. As distrust is the mark of a narrow intellect or a bad heart, so a readiness to believe in the ability of others is not only a characteristic of able men, but it is also the secret charm which calls around them helpers and followers. Hence, a strong man who loves his work is a better educator than a half-hearted professor who carries whole libraries in his head.

To bring together in familiar and daily life a number of young men, chosen for the brightness of their minds and an eager yearning for knowledge, is to create an atmosphere of intellectual warmth and light, which invigorates and inspires the master, while it stimulates his disciples. In such company it will not be difficult to form teachers. But will it be possible to find young men who will consent, when after years of study they have finally reached the priesthood, to continue in a higher institution the arduous and confining labors to the end of which they have looked as to the beginning of a new life? In other lands such students are found, and if with us there is a tendency to rush with precipitancy and insufficient preparation to whatever work we may have chosen, this is but a proof of the need of special efforts to restrain an ardor which springs from weakness and not from strength. Haste is a mark of immaturity. He who is certain of himself and master of his tools, knows that he is able, and neither hurries nor worries, but works and waits. The rank weed shoots up in a day and as quickly dies; but the long-growing olive-tree stands from century to century, and drops from its gently waving boughs ripe fruit through the quiet autumn air. The Church endures forever; and we American Catholics, in the midst of our rapidly-moving and ever-changing society, should be the first to learn to temper energy with the patient strength which gives the courage to toil and wait through a long life, if so we make ourselves worthy to speak some fit word or do some needful deed. And to whom shall this lesson first be taught if not to the clerics, whose natural endowments single them out as future leaders of Catholic thought and enterprise; and where can this lesson so well be learned as in a school whose standard of intellectual excellence shall be the highest?

While we look, therefore, to the founding of a true university, we will begin, as the university of Paris began in the twelfth century, and as the present university of Louvain began fifty years ago, with a national school of philosophy and theology, which will form the central faculty of a complete educational organism. Around this, the other faculties will take their places, in due course of time; and so the beginning which we make will grow, until like the seed planted in the earth, it shall wear the bloomy crown of its own development.

And though the event be less than our hope, though even failure be the outcome, is it not better to fail than not to attempt a worthy work which might be ours? Only they who do nothing derive comfort from the mistakes of others; and the saying that a blunder is worse than a crime is doubtless true for those who have no other measure of worth and success than the conventional standards of a superficial public opinion. We at least know—

> "There lives a Judge
> To whose all-pondering mind a noble aim
> Faithfully kept is as a noble deed;
> In whose pure sight all virtue doth succeed."

THE END.

9 789361 381867

Printed by Libri Plureos GmbH in Hamburg,
Germany